Mi Padre

Mi Padre

Mexican Immigrant Fathers and Their Children's Education

Sarah Gallo

Foreword by Guadalupe Valdés

TEACHERS COLLEGE PRESS

TEACHERS COLLEGE | COLUMBIA UNIVERSITY
NEW YORK AND LONDON

Published by Teachers College Press, 1234 Amsterdam Avenue, New York, NY 10027

Cover design by Sarah Martin. Cover photo by Aldo Murillo / iStock by Getty Images.

Library of Congress Cataloging-in-Publication Data

Names: Mayorga-Gallo, Sarah, author.
Title: Mi padre : Mexican immigrant fathers and their children's education / Sarah Gallo.
Description: New York, NY : Teachers College Press, [2017] | Includes bibliographical references and index.
Identifiers: LCCN 2016055473 | ISBN 9780807756737 (pbk. : alk. paper)
Subjects: LCSH: Children of immigrants—Education—United States—Case studies. | Mexican American children—Education—Case studies. | Community and school—United States—Case studies. | Father and child—United States—Case studies.
Classification: LCC LC3746 .M39 2017 | DDC 371.829/68073--dc23
LC record available at https://lccn.loc.gov/2016055473

ISBN 978-0-8077-5673-7 (paper)
ISBN 978-0-8077-7564-6 (ebook)

Printed on acid-free paper
Manufactured in the United States of America

24   23   22   21   20   19   18   17   8   7   6   5   4   3   2   1

Contents

Foreword

I am both honored and delighted to have been asked by Sarah Gallo to write the foreword for one of the most outstanding books that I have read on families and schools in a very long time. This volume is excellently written and focuses on the key issues that involve relationships between American teachers and the parents of Mexican immigrant-origin children.

Over several years, an increasing number of scholars have echoed my own arguments (Valdés, 1996) about the shortcomings of many well-meaning *family education, family involvement,* and *family engagement* efforts that focus on changing the everyday child-rearing practices of Mexican immigrant families. With the best of intentions, both scholars and educators have dismissed generations of culturally informed practices that families bring with them to this country and have sought to teach them "parenting skills" (typical of Anglo-American, middle-class families) that they credit with producing children who are "ready to learn."

This volume directly questions these widely accepted assumptions. Drawing from a 3-year ethnography carried out in Pennsylvania in an elementary school that served Mexican immigrant families, Gallo proposes a framework, termed *humanizing family engagement,* that has as its purpose helping teachers to build relationships with families (including fathers) across levels of difference to improve the schooling of Latin@ children.

The focus on fathers is central to this work. Gallo's book adds to our understanding of the gendered nature of parent–teacher relations by sharing the experiences of well-intentioned educators as they interacted (and failed to interact) with Mexican *fathers.* She offers the reader a clear view of the ways in which male Latino, immigrant parents (often stereotyped as *macho,* uneducated, and undocumented) were routinely made invisible in schools. In parent–teacher conferences in which Gallo served as an interpreter, for example, teachers did not address fathers when the mother was present. Even when these fathers were actively engaged in their children's lives and in supporting their development and both school and life learning in numerous ways, teachers could not see beyond the sets of activities that have currently been identified as desirable *parent involvement* (e.g., helping with homework as directed by the teacher). They could not recognize the range of ways that caring family members support children's schooling.

In describing Mexican immigrant fathers, Gallo seeks to move beyond stereotypes to *humantypes*, that is, to views of human beings that are layered, complex, and contradictory. Gallo's presentation of the fathers and their children is detailed and nuanced and invites the reader to see inside the families themselves. It also provides descriptions of the various ways in which teachers' interactions with fathers can be improved and of the steps that can be taken by educators in gaining ideological clarity, that is, in developing the ability to question their own beliefs and ideologies about race, class, power, privilege, and education itself.

Aware that most young teachers are not currently prepared by their pre-service programs to problematize the ideological basis of the practices valued in schools and to understand how and why these favored practices are the product of class, education, and white privilege, Gallo provides, in every chapter, what she calls *Pedagogical Takeaways* and *Reflection Questions*. Teachers are guided in their journey toward humanizing family engagement by a step-by-step, chapter-by-chapter set of suggested activities that will help them examine what counts, increase their own learning about families who do not have those advantages, and reflect on their own values and beliefs.

Gallo tells us that the book is not intended as a how-to guide. And indeed, it is much more than that. This well-crafted ethnography will, as the author intends, raise awareness about alternatives to current narrow models of parent involvement and parent education and allow readers to enter the lives of Mexican fathers and their children. Importantly, also, in the same spirit of Gopnik's (2016) strong critique of the widely accepted notion of "parenting" as a goal-directed set of activities that "good" parents must and should do to produce successful adults, this volume specifically guides teachers in developing strategies to enact humanizing pedagogies within the constraints of their schools and classrooms. She encourages them (1) to understand that education is political, (2) to develop ideological clarity about what and how they teach, (3) to develop interpersonal relationships with students and to learn from them, and (4) to look for like-minded colleagues to form a supportive community in which they can find "wiggle room" in the curriculum and organize against harmful policies and practices.

For me, this is an essential book that should be added to the reading list of all current and future educators. Researchers, teachers, and teacher educators of many types and backgrounds will learn much from this insightful book. Gallo provides all of us a vision for understanding the strengths, the challenges, and the determination of immigrant families and for supporting their ongoing efforts to create a garden (a protective and nurturing space) (Gopnik, 2016) in which their children can bloom as competent, intelligent, and good human beings.

—Guadalupe Valdés
Stanford University

REFERENCES

Gopnik, A. (2016). *The gardener and the carpenter*. New York, NY: Farrar, Straus & Giroux.

Valdés, G. (1996). *Con respeto: Bridging the distances between culturally diverse parents and schools: An ethnographic portrait*. New York, NY: Teachers College Press.

Acknowledgments

This book was the result of many people's generosity and support. My ethnographic research in Marshall, Pennsylvania, began under the guidance of Kathryn Howard and throughout the years was further enhanced by my mentors at Penn, including Betsy Rymes, Stanton Wortham, Nancy Hornberger, and Kathy Hall. The fieldwork and analyses that informed this book were supported by a National Science Foundation dissertation improvement grant in cultural anthropology and a dissertation fellowship from the National Academy of Education and the Spencer Foundation.

I am indebted to Valerie Kinloch for her advice and encouragement in pursuing this book, and to Tim San Pedro for his insightful feedback. I am grateful to Michiko Hikida, who dedicated many hours of her summer to provide thoughtful feedback on this entire manuscript, and to Millie Gort, who offered important suggestions for Chapters 1 and 3.

Thank you to my academic partner in (good) crime, Holly Link, whose presence permeates these pages. Since 2008, Holly and I have collaborated on many projects in Marshall, and some of the implications in this book, most notably in Chapter 6, were informed by our joint research and publications. Thank you also for providing constructive feedback on this entire manuscript. I am honored to be able to research, write, collaborate, and continually learn with you.

Finally, this book is dedicated to *las familias y l@s maestr@s de* Marshall, Pennsylvania. Thank you for opening your homes, classrooms, and lives to me.

Preface

It was a summer evening in Pennsylvania as I sat on the couch with Dan[1] and Jessica, an immigrant couple from Guerrero, Mexico. We were in their small apartment four blocks from Grant Elementary School, and their children were watching soccer on the television in another room. Dan held up a photograph of me and my wife, and as he pointed to each of us he asked with a caring smile, "Which one's the man?" He was trying to make sense of my marriage—as a woman—to another woman. I had just shared a part of myself that I had initially kept from most of the Mexican immigrant families I worked with during my 7 years in Marshall, Pennsylvania. I have a wife.

I had been afraid to share this part of my life with families in 2010, afraid that they would view me through a deficit lens based upon pathologizing stereotypes about Lesbian, Gay, Bisexual, Transgender, and Queer (LGBTQ) people. My fear was that they would no longer know me as a unique, idiosyncratic person, but simply as a label—*gay*. Yet instead of creating distance between us, my sharing resulted in a heartfelt 2-hour conversation about gender identification, sexual orientation, and discrimination. I was one of the first openly gay people Dan had known well, and he wanted to understand my perspectives and experiences better. As Dan quickly highlighted, as a *hispano* (Hispanic person) in the United States, he knew what it is like to be discriminated against, and he tried not to discriminate against others. In retrospect, I realize how my fears about coming out share some similarities with students' and caregivers' experiences revealing their undocumented status. Dan's reaction—in which he took the time to ask questions and authentically listen, rather than quickly changing the subject because of his uncertainty of how to navigate the delicate topic of sexual orientation—taught me about learning across difference.

Dan and I came into this conversation as two people of the same age with different life experiences. At that time, I was a childless, nonreligious, gay, White, English-Spanish bilingual U.S. citizen completing my PhD. He was a straight, Catholic, Spanish-dominant Mexican immigrant father with a middle school education who served in the Mexican military before migrating to the United States with his hometown sweetheart. In Marshall, he dedicated himself to his three children while working two jobs, working professionally as a DJ, and dabbling in the arts. Through this, and many other conversations over the years, we sought out ways to learn from and with each other across differences such as gender, national origin, race, class, religion, sexual orientation, and documentation status. Dan, and the other fathers who inform this book, taught me a great deal about (in)visibility, trust, schooling, and education.

This book is about Mexican immigrant fathers and their children's education. It grew from a dissonance that I came to recognize while working with families and schools in Marshall for several years: Mexican immigrant fathers like Dan were very involved in their children's lives and schooling, yet their contributions went widely unrecognized within local schools, the research literature, and the media. In schools, Mexican immigrant fathers tended to be overlooked; in public spaces saturated with messages about "illegal" immigrants, they were positioned as likely "criminals;" and they were hyper-visible for local law enforcement. Yet *invisible* in these larger circulating stereotypes were the details and familial effects of targeting Latino immigrant men for minor infractions. A common thread throughout these instances is that the racialization of the category of "Mexican men" makes their roles as educators and fathers invisible. The effects of their racialization shape their children's educational lives, including how educators come to understand fathers as involved in their children's schooling.

In this book, I focus on Mexican immigrant fathers and their children's educational experiences to propose a framework that I term *humanizing family engagement*. *Mi Padre* theorizes how diverse caregivers and educators can learn across their differences in support of students' schooling. The following inquiries guide the research presented in this book:

1. How do Mexican immigrant fathers contribute to their children's schooling in traditional and innovative ways? How are their pedagogies of the home recognized, built upon, or overlooked by their children's teachers? How might they be better leveraged to inform classroom-based practices? These questions frame Part I (Chapters 1–4) of the book.

2. How do documentation status and deportation-based immigration practices affect Mexican immigrant children, their families, and their elementary school teachers? This question frames Part II (Chapters 5–7) of the book.

3. How might humanizing family engagement, in which fathers and teachers build authentic relationships across levels of difference, help improve schooling for Latin@ students? This question frames the discussion, reflection questions, and pedagogical takeaways that are integrated into each chapter.

In this book, I illustrate how overall well-intentioned educators had few opportunities to foster humanizing relationships with immigrant fathers. The humanizing family engagement framework presented here is a result arising from the research and helps reveal the range of sociocultural and linguistic resources that students brought from home. In addition, it provides a lens to understand the successes as well as the missed opportunities in which teachers inadvertently overlooked or misinterpreted fathers' contributions to their children's schooling. Through explorations of students' educational lives with their fathers, the book provides a window into a wider range of educational practices that educators often are not aware of in school that could be built upon to support students' schooling.

My aim is to improve schooling for children through examples of how caregivers' pedagogies of the home can be better recognized and leveraged for academic success. Examples of fathers' educational experiences with their children provide a vehicle to move past labels, such as *Mexican, immigrant, illegal,* or *undocumented,* that are often used to categorize and dehumanize men from Mexico. I show how fathers' pedagogies offered children lessons on how to develop biliteracy, examine critically, strategically resist, and reshape the story of who they are in the United States. The process illustrated in this book matters for schooling because it provides educators with critical insights on the importance of designing classroom pedagogies that can leverage and build upon the language, literacy, and experiential knowledge that diverse students bring to their school-based learning.

AUDIENCES

This book is written with several audiences in mind. The primary audience includes inservice and preservice teachers who may work with Latin@ immigrant families and their children or other minoritized populations. It shines a spotlight on the heterogeneous resources that one type of diverse caregivers, Mexican immigrant fathers, brings to their children's education and through their complex experiences offers opportunities to question stereotypes and explore the traditional and innovative ways in which they contribute to their children's schooling. A second audience consists of administrators or policymakers who work with public schools, and who are interested in better understanding the educational resources and realities that many Latin@ students and families bring to schooling. A final important audience includes graduate students who are interested in long-term school- or family-based ethnographic research. Appendix B provides further insight on the research methodology.

A NOTE ON LANGUAGE

There are always multiple ways to name things, each carrying with it a different history and set of assumptions. Here, I explain my choices around some of the key terminology used in this book.

Translations: Families from this study used English and Spanish in dynamic ways, and many of the interactions represented here unfolded in Spanish, or through translanguaging, the use of Spanish and English (García, 2009). At times, I include the original language(s) spoken, with an English translation. Because of space limitations, there are other times where I provide the English translation directly.

Latin@: I purposefully use the term *Latin@* when referring to a group comprised of people of Latin American heritage of various genders. There are many different ways to refer to Latin@s (for example, *Latino, Latina/o, Latinx*), each carrying different connotations. *Latino* comes from Spanish, with the *o* referencing a masculine ending, which many argue carries an unfair bias for those who identify as female. Throughout this book, I instead use *Latin@*, as the @ includes masculine and feminine genders. I recognize that for some readers the term *Latin@* may be new and may require getting used to, but I select this term for its inclusivity.

Yet there are specific instances in which I do not use *Latin@* as well. In self-descriptions participants often described themselves as Mexican or *hispano*, not Latin@. All focal families in this study were of Mexican origin, and the Latin@ population was estimated at approximately 80% Mexican in Marshall. My use of *Mexican* rather than *Latin@* is not because I conflate the two. I refer to the individual participants as Mexican, because this is how they identified. I use the term *Latin@* to engage the broader scholarship in Latin@ education.

Illegal versus undocumented: I do not refer to those without official U.S. documentation as *illegals*. I believe that no human being is illegal, and that drawing upon such terms perpetuates notions that those without U.S. documentation are less important, or less human. Although it is imperfect, I prefer the term *undocumented*, because it moves away from notions of criminality or foreign otherness (as with the term *illegal alien*). *Undocumented* instead focuses on the structural processes of being able to officially access government documents, such as visas, needed to lawfully reside within a certain territory.

Machismo and macho: *Machismo* references male chauvinism and exaggerated masculinity. Gutmann (1996) illustrates how a few early studies described Mexican origin men in this way, overemphasizing the negative aspects of machismo. Gutmann emphasizes how in the United States the term *machismo* has an explicitly racist history, as it "has been associated with negative character traits not among men in general, but specifically among Mexican, Mexican American, and Latin American men" (p. 227). Men from Mexico, in particular, are often stereotyped as engaging in machismo, or being *macho*. Associating men with machismo deprives all men, but particularly Latinos, of part of their humanity.

Minoritized: Following McCarty (2002), I use the term *minoritized* rather than *minority* to reflect the power relations and processes by which some groups are marginalized within the larger society. Throughout this book, I reference students who are not from White, middle class families as *minoritized*, *diverse*, and *nonmainstream*. Students from Mexican immigrant families fall within these broader labels. I use broader labels because humanizing family engagement approaches would be beneficial not just for teachers working with Mexican immigrant families, but for those working with families from all minoritized groups.

Parent/caregiver: I use the terms *parent* and *caregiver* interchangeably. When using these terms, I mean an open category that references any caring adult or family member who contributes to a child's education.

Emergent bilingual: Drawing from Ofelia García (2009), I too refer to students who live and learn in more than one language as *emergent bilinguals*. Rather than labels such as *English language learners (ELL)* or *English as a Second Language (ESL) student* that prioritize the importance of English, I use *emergent bilingual* to highlight the potential for students to develop bilingualism if given the proper supports.

Part I

FROM STEREOTYPES TO HUMANTYPES AND LEVERAGING DIFFERENCE

Chapter 1

From Stereotypes to Humantypes

It was a wintery Sunday afternoon in Marshall, Pennsylvania, as 7-year-old Abi, the child of Mexican immigrants, stood talking with her father, Mateo, and mother, Susana, in the kitchen of their two-bedroom apartment. As her parents prepared dinner, Abi began to conduct a mock interview in Spanish in which she gauged her father's perspectives about men's domestic responsibilities. Susana modeled an opening interview question for her daughter, encouraging Abi to ask her father, "What do you think about men who cook at home?" He responded that it was "cool" and the way it should be, because household responsibilities were not solely for women. Following her parents' lead, Abi stepped into the role of interviewer.

As Susana filmed, Abi and Mateo engaged in this faux interview. He followed his daughter's cues as he taught her about interviewing, simultaneously performing the roles of knowledgeable teacher and caring father. Grabbing a nearby bottle of hot sauce to use as an impromptu microphone, he warmly instructed Abi on proper interview techniques. Like a skilled teacher, he modeled interview-appropriate linguistic forms such as "*¿y qué opina Usted?*" ("And what is your opinion, sir?"), which draw upon structures of politeness in Spanish. Through this playful interview, in which 2nd-grader Abi embodied the role of a reporter, Abi and her father also broached difficult themes related to stereotypes based on national origin. In a put-on newscaster voice, Abi held the faux microphone up to her father's mouth and asked what he was cooking, to which he responded, "Mexican-style steak." In an exaggerated tone of snobbery, Abi added, "Eww, I'm not Mexican; I'm American." Mateo pushed back against this subtle anti-Mexican statement by jokingly referencing the newscaster persona that Abi had taken on as "*Gabacha*," a somewhat undesirable term for a White girl. Abi, keeping with her news reporter role, drew upon her quick wit and retorted, "I'm not like the Mexicans who don't bathe." Without skipping a beat, Mateo pulled her in close for a hug and jocularly encouraged her to smell his armpit, causing the entire family to erupt in laughter. Susana drew upon her resources in Spanish and English as she commented, "*Es así la vida de mi familia.* (This is what my family's life is like.) Everyday it's the same."

PEDAGOGIES OF THE HOME

Through this routine interaction, Abi's parents—and Mateo, in particular— were involved in their daughter's education in important ways. They engaged in what Dolores Delgado Bernal (2001) terms "pedagogies of the home": home-based learning that sometimes overlaps with school-based learning, but also equips minoritized students with additional tools and cultural knowledge that "helps them survive and succeed in an educational system that often excludes and silences them" (p. 623). Like the English medium literacy activities in Abi's 2nd-grade classroom, Mateo developed his daughter's awareness of how to use language and linguistic forms in appropriate ways for specific audiences in Spanish. Through the common practice of cooking dinner for his family and voicing his beliefs that couples should share household responsibilities, he countered narrow images of Latino immigrant men who are often portrayed as machos uninvolved in their family's lives. He and Susana strove to flexibly model for their children how both parents can take on household and income-earning responsibilities in ways that pushed against traditional gender norms.

Finally, Abi and Mateo were aware of deficit-based stereotypes about people of Mexican origin: that they are dirty, do not bathe, and that many people may prefer to identify as "American" rather than "Mexican" if being Mexican means being associated with these negative characteristics. Abi was proud of her Mexican heritage, and when not taking on the pretend role of a reporter she enthusiastically identified as *Mexicana*. Yet through this role-play, she revealed her awareness regarding common stereotypes that were often used against Mexican immigrants like her and her family. Just as Mateo often did through his verbal artistry in Spanish, here he drew upon humor and linguistic nuance through the term *Gabacha* (White girl) to position being from the United States as less desirable, while simultaneously placing being Mexican in a positive light. Through humor he converted a difficult topic—detrimental stereotypes based on country of origin—into a speakable theme that would prepare his children to counter deficit images of Latin@s that they would encounter in the media, communities, and potentially in school.

This routine interaction illustrates the ways that Mateo engaged in an array of parent involvement practices that included more traditional forms of parent involvement (such as language and literacy development) as well as less recognized forms of parent involvement (such as preparing his children to combat discrimination based on their Mexican heritage). This book centers on the educational lives of young students like Abi across home and school contexts and their Mexican immigrant fathers who were involved in their schooling in traditional and innovative ways. Mateo did not engage in these involvement practices alone, but did so alongside his wife, as they fluidly navigated work, home, and school life as an immigrant family in Pennsylvania.

Through examples of the dynamic ways that educators sometimes recognized or overlooked the educational resources that fathers contributed to their children's education, I propose a framework that I term *humanizing family engagement*. This framework, which emerged from a 3-year ethnographic project, invites readers to imagine ways to productively foster family–school relationships that build upon the range of resources that young people and their families bring to schooling. This is true for families from Mexican immigrant backgrounds—the focus of this book—as well as more broadly for families from other minoritized backgrounds who do not identify as mainstream, or White and middle class. I argue that teachers and schools should move away from narrow approaches to parent involvement and instead approach family–school relationships as humanizing engagement. Humanizing family engagement provides a lens to pedagogically leverage a wider range of educational resources that diverse students and families bring to their classrooms. This can help support positive educational trajectories for diverse students.

FAMILY–SCHOOL RELATIONSHIPS IN THE NEW LATINO DIASPORA

Parent Involvement and Family–School Engagement

Parent involvement is based on the premise that students will be more academically successful if educators and caregivers work together to support their learning. In most U.S. schools, this often translates into parents' help with school-sanctioned tasks such as homework, attendance at school events such as parent–teacher conferences, and volunteering for the school. As Angela Calabrese Barton and colleagues (2004) argue, most parent involvement policies and practices examine how parents do—or do not— embody a set list of practices that count as parent involvement. Parents, especially those from minoritized backgrounds, who do not eagerly engage in these types of practices in recognizable ways are often positioned by educators (often on a subconscious level) as not caring about their children's education. Fabienne Doucet (2011a) argues that most parent involvement practices in schools exclude parents from diverse backgrounds, and that authentic family–school collaboration requires rethinking perspectives and rituals related to parent involvement. This book takes up this charge and provides a vehicle to question and reimagine what parent involvement can be, especially when engaging with students and families who bring different knowledges and resources to their children's schooling.

Drawing from Barton et al. (2004), I use the term *engagement*, rather than *involvement*, to move away from a set list of activities that traditionally count as parent involvement (homework help and so forth). Engagement instead encourages educators to examine caregivers' real world practices to understand how they see themselves as contributing to children's educational lives. I also emphasize *family–school* engagement, rather than *parent–teacher* engagement, because it encompasses the range of family members and school-based individuals who support a child's schooling. It also highlights the mutual responsibilities that people from families and schools have to successfully support a child's education; the onus is not on families or teachers alone.

Thus, in addition to *what* gets recognized as parent involvement, this book offers a canvas to explore *who* gets recognized as engaged in children's schooling. In the opening vignette, Abi clearly views her father as a knowledgeable expert, and in my years working with Mexican immigrant fathers and their children in both homes and schools, this was common. However, Mexican immigrant fathers' participation in their children's schooling was often invisible in local educational institutions and, arguably, the mainstream educational world overall. An important body of scholarship has contested the deficit-based assumption that Latin@ families don't care about their children's education, yet this research tends to focus on Latina mothers' practices (e.g., Dyrness, 2011; Valdés, 1996). Such an emphasis risks reifying notions of family–school engagement as women's work.

Building from foundational work by scholars such as Gerardo López (2001), this book uniquely privileges the perspectives and experiences of fathers of Mexican heritage, which are often absent from the growing body of literature on Latin@ families' engagement in schooling. This is not to overlook mothers' important contributions, as students' mothers also played roles in supporting their children's schooling. Instead, it shifts the spotlight to fathers' educational practices within the contexts of their families' homes and their children's schools. Through a focus on Mexican immigrant fathers, this book pushes readers to recognize gendered assumptions of family–school engagement practices. It offers a framework and examples to consider what can be gained by recognizing the range of ways in which caring family members support students' schooling. It also pushes educators to consider additional educational practices that are not present in their classrooms, and how they could incorporate these pedagogies of the home into school-based learning.

A Community of the New Latino Diaspora

This book grew from a 3-year ethnography on the elementary school experiences of children from Mexican immigrant families that I conducted between 2008 and 2011 in the town of Marshall, Pennsylvania. Marshall is a suburb of approximately 35,000 people that has become home to thousands of Latin@ immigrants over the past 2 decades. From 1990 to 2010, the Latin@ population increased from 3% to 28%—about a 900% increase. Most immigrant families from this study lived alongside African American neighbors in the economically depressed downtown area that offered inexpensive housing. This housing was near a thoroughfare with predominantly Mexican businesses, such as restaurants, small markets, and variety stores. During the day, the streets in this part of town were usually lively with people from the local neighborhood running errands, kids playing in side streets, or people talking with friends as they sat on their front stoop. Yet crime was also a real part of students' neighborhoods, and most families were mindful of being outside after dark. Marshall and its surrounding suburbs were also racially and economically segregated. This meant that most members of the middle class, including most educators, lived in surrounding suburbs equipped with malls, high-end organic grocery stores, and lower crime rates. Because their friendship networks and daily routines rarely led them into downtown Marshall, educators did not often have the opportunity to see the communities that formed the backdrop of students' lives.

Just as community demographics changed, so did school district enrollments: From 1987 to 2011, the Latin@ student enrollment increased from 2% to 25%, with a large concentration of Latin@ students in the elementary grades. The study's focal school, Grant Elementary, was located in Marshall's downtown. A Title I school, with approximately 95% of its students receiving free or reduced-price lunch, Grant Elementary worked with more than 400 students in grades K–4, with relatively equal numbers of African American and Latin@ students. Families in the study came from the cohort of students who began kindergarten in 2008. Most of the Latin@ students were born in the United States to Mexican immigrant parents, or arrived from Mexico prior to kindergarten. The majority lived in mixed-status families in which younger family members had U.S. documentation, while other family members did not.

Similar to current profiles of teachers outside urban areas (Ingersoll & Merrill, 2012), teachers at Grant Elementary were almost entirely White middle-class women. Teachers were generally welcoming to newcomer students and their families. There were no bilingual education programs for elementary school children in Marshall, and all instruction at Grant was conducted in English. Most teachers at Grant Elementary and throughout the district were monolingual English speakers, but Grant teachers viewed children's use of Spanish with one another as an important resource in the classroom.

The shifting population of Grant Elementary reflected national trends in public school enrollments: By 2014, students of color outnumbered White students in public schools (National Center for Education Statistics, 2016). In addition, by 2011 one in four children in U.S. public schools was an immigrant or the U.S.-born child of an immigrant, and by 2050, that number is anticipated to be one in three (Passel, 2011). These shifting demographics have led to the most racially and ethnically diverse school population in the history of the country (Passel, 2011). Students are also growing up in households in which languages other than English are spoken, and 9% of the public school population receives English language supports to facilitate their learning in English medium schooling (National Center for Education Statistics, 2015).

It is also estimated that at least three-quarters of public schools serve students who qualify for English language supports (U.S. Department of Justice, n.d.), and in 2010 it was estimated that approximately 75% of emergent bilingual students came from Spanish-speaking families (García & Kleifgen, 2010). This is partially a reflection of new immigrant settlement patterns that have shifted since the 1990s. By the beginning of the 21st century, newcomers from an array of backgrounds had become important parts of rural, suburban, and urban communities across the nation. This is true for Latin@s, who—in addition to living in long-established Latin@ communities in places such as Texas and California—have increasingly settled as families in newer locations, including North Carolina, Nebraska, and Pennsylvania. This demographic shift is sometimes called the new Latino diaspora (Wortham, Murillo, & Hamann, 2002).

Changing school populations mean that educators are likely to teach students who bring a wider range of knowledges and experiences to their classrooms. Many educational scholars have demonstrated that children develop resources across contexts of learning, and that young people from minoritized backgrounds are more academically successful when educators incorporate these resources into their schooling (Heath, 1983; Moll, Amanti, Neff, & González, 1992; Valenzuela, 1999). For many educators, this means that it is beneficial to get to know students, families, and knowledges that differ from their own, which requires learning across difference. This book is an examination of how teachers in a community undergoing demographic change navigated family–school relationships, and how a humanizing approach can better support educators and families to guide students' positive educational trajectories.

HUMANTYPES AND STEREOTYPES

Through the complex educational experiences of Mexican immigrant fathers and their children, in this book I aim to represent *humantypes* rather than stereotypes. Eve Tuck (2009) described humantypes as "layered in composition and meaning . . . determined to show complexity and often reveal contradiction" (p. 418). She emphasized that "stereotype images depicted African American people as subhuman, as objects, as jokes, as static. Conversely . . . humantype(s) . . . portrayed African American people as having pasts and presents and futures" (p. 418). Stereotypes often rely on static images of those who are considered "other," and are created and perpetuated by people who have limited experiences personally getting to know individuals from a given group. Humantypes can only emerge once we get to know one another as complex, multifaceted, and dynamic individuals.

In the media and larger national imagination, there are no shortages of stereotypes for Latino immigrant men. As the 2016 presidential elections with Donald Trump blatantly illustrated, Mexican nationals are talked about as *illegals*, *rapists*, *killers*, and affiliated with drug crime. This is not new, and many scholars have documented how Latino men have historically been labeled dangerous criminals, chauvinistic machos, or like animals that are invading the United States (Chávez, 2008; Santa Ana, 1999). Such flat, two-dimensional images have the cumulative effect of dehumanizing Latinos. In contrast, this book offers a window into men of Mexican heritage as caring fathers and husbands as they engage in educational activities with their children across home and school spaces. It offers insights into fathers such as Ignacio, whom 2nd-grader Martina talked about through joyful tears as "always there for me," and Cristián, who wanted to be his daughter's "Superman always. Her Superdaddy." I seek to move away from pathologizing narratives that often frame the research and media on Latino immigrant men to instead examine how individual fathers and children drew upon their dynamic range of resources to meet their educational goals.

This approach does not mean that I overlook the challenging experiences in their lives, such as the ways that a parent's undocumented status shapes educational realities. As immigration practices shifted in Marshall, there were many instances in which documentation status created real challenges for families, children, and educators. Yet, in broaching these topics, I aim to show their textured complexities and to acknowledge the caring and thoughtful ways in which parents prepared their children to navigate such contexts. I believe that teacher educators need to foster conversation regarding documentation status as a type of difference to better prepare teachers to recognize and build upon students' immigration experiences—both the positive and challenging—when students bring them to their classroom learning (see Gallo, 2014; Gallo & Link, 2015, 2016). Humantypes require us to think about the terms and the associated images involved when we talk about people, such as the use of terms such as *undocumented* rather than *illegal*. In this book, I aim to delve into these complexities, rather than silence them.

MY ROLES

As I describe below, I first met families in Marshall in 2006, and in 2008 I began working on ethnographic projects within Grant Elementary School that focused on a cohort of kindergarten students and their families from Mexico. This study included weekly participant observation in their kindergarten classrooms, video recording of routine activities, and interviews at home and school. It also involved close interaction with dozens of families and educators. My long-term presence as a bilingual adult led to trusting relationships, which were essential to discussing topics such as gendered family roles and immigration with students, families, and educators.

I say that these experiences are *re-presentations* rather than simply *presentations* to emphasize the ways that my own roles and subjectivities shape how I experienced, understood, analyzed, and reproduced them (Kirkland, 2013). This is true for all of us. I am a non-Latina bilingual who has spent most of my adult life living in Latin America and working with Latin@ immigrants and schools. Although I shared many of the same linguistic resources as the families I worked with, we often differed in terms of our nationalities, race, income, level of formal education, gender, sexuality, and documentation status. In many ways, this book is an example of the kind of learning across difference that I continually experience. As I spent time getting to know families and educators, I tried to reciprocate their generosity as they welcomed me into their homes and classrooms. I regularly interpreted for teachers, answered their questions about working with immigrant families while maintaining families' confidentiality, and helped in classrooms. I also helped parents navigate schooling, technology, health care, and immigration questions. For several families dealing with immigration issues, I was one of the few bilingual adults and U.S. citizens they knew well and felt they could trust.

As a researcher, I was afforded opportunities to spend extensive time with families and students across contexts, which permitted the space for us to get to know one another across our many levels of difference. I recognize that the wonderful educators I worked with for 7 years at Grant Elementary School, who faced increasing demands on their time to meet accountability measures, rarely had extensive access to these same kinds of opportunities. Yet I also noticed the various ways that some teachers came to build relationships with students' parents, which helped them recognize the educational resources that caregivers contributed to their children's schooling. This led me to envision how family–school engagement policies, practices, and approaches could better leverage diverse families' educational resources.

RESEARCH METHODOLOGY

I first met families and educators in Marshall in 2006, as a doctoral student. I began volunteering as an interpreter for parent–teacher conferences at Grant Elementary and as a teacher for a family educational program within a bilingual service agency, where Martina and Princess were preschoolers. In 2008, I began ethnographic studies at Grant Elementary with a cohort of kindergarten students and their families from Mexico. I continued working with this cohort of students in 1st grade and then through this study, which was conducted during students' 2nd-grade year (2010–2011).[1] By 2010, I also knew educators at Grant Elementary well, as I had served as an interpreter at family–school events for 4 years, had led several professional development trainings, had supported initiatives to foster collaborations with Latin@ immigrant families, and had conducted weekly participant observation in classrooms. Although the relationships I established with families and educators were necessary for the success of this study, the findings presented in this book focus on the data collected during students' 2nd-grade year.

I invited seven Mexican immigrant families to participate in this study in order to better understand how fathers were engaged in their children's educational lives. Five of these families are centrally featured in this book. Over the years, I was struck by the relative invisibility of immigrant fathers within the research literature and within educators' talk in local schools, which stood in stark contrast to the extensive engagement many Mexican immigrant fathers had in their children's lives. I did not view these fathers as "more engaged" than other fathers—I was interested in their practices because the fathers appeared to be engaged in their children's educational lives in diverse ways. Several of the students and families I had worked with on previous ethnographic studies and others I had gotten to know through district-based initiatives with Latin@ immigrant parents. All of them agreed to participate.

HUMANIZING FAMILY ENGAGEMENT

An in-depth look at children's educational experiences with their Mexican immigrant fathers across contexts of learning provides a canvas for readers to explore the potential of humanizing relationships with those who differ from themselves. Humanizing family engagement invites readers to grapple with the importance of learning from and with diverse families, to engage with the political aspects of education, and to consider the educational benefits of recognizing a wider range of practices that count as involvement. It is beneficial for educators to approach family–school relationships as humanizing family engagement because it provides a lens to better recognize and build upon the range of educational resources that minoritized students and families bring to school.

Asset-Based Pedagogies

The humanizing family engagement framework falls under the broader umbrella of asset-based pedagogies. Asset-based pedagogies are founded on the belief that children develop knowledges and resources across contexts of learning (for example, school, homes, and communities), and that young people from minoritized backgrounds will be more academically successful if educators build upon the knowledges and resources that children bring to school (Gay, 2000; Ladson-Billings, 1995; Moll et al., 1992). As Paris and Alim (2014) highlight, "these pedagogies repositioned the linguistic, literate, and cultural practices of working class communities—specifically poor communities of color—as resources and assets to honor, explore, and extend" (pp. 87–88). Much of the earlier work by groundbreaking scholars focused on the experiences, learning styles, and cultural identities of African American students and pushed educators to develop strategies that would respond to students' cultural identities. Moll and colleagues' (1992) work on "funds of knowledge," or the "historically accumulated and culturally developed bodies of knowledge and skills essential for household and individual functioning and well-being" (p. 133), provided an important linkage between home-based and school-based knowledges for immigrant populations in particular. Through this work, they challenged the notion that valuable knowledges were only created and learned within mainstream schooling, where the language and literacy resources of White middle class families were most valued. They pushed educators to step outside of their classrooms—into students' homes and communities—to take on the role of learners in order to design and implement classroom curricula based upon the cultural, community, and family-based resources that minoritized students bring to their schools.

These earlier approaches laid an important foundation to question the narrow range of resources and ways of learning that are often incorporated into schooling. Yet they have been critiqued for how they have come to be applied in essentializing ways that do not adequately capture the range of experiences and hybrid identities that are part of today's classrooms. Applications of culturally relevant pedagogies have tended to assume that all students from a given group (such as African Americans) share core characteristics. This overlooks within-group differences and the ways individual experiences shape their learning (Gutiérrez & Rogoff, 2003; Paris & Alim, 2014). In practice, dynamic frameworks such as funds of knowledge have been reduced to a shorthand for celebrating static special events from students' countries of origin, without creating spaces to understand the true lived realities in students' lives, such as being a member of an undocumented family. Although the originators of these asset-based pedagogies did not intend such essentializing and static applications, this is how their work has often been used in educational research and settings. This book instead focuses on in-group differences and the dynamic ways that fathers, children, and educators navigate them. It provides a window into the dynamic and heterogeneous lives and learning of individual families to begin to develop this critical awareness. It aims to raise educators' awareness about the ways they form interpersonal relationships with people who differ from themselves in order to understand the unique repertoire of resources that families bring to schooling.

Humanizing Family Engagement Framework

What are often called humanizing pedagogies, like other asset-based pedagogies, seek to foster schooling that critically examines and builds upon the sociohistorical realities in diverse students' lives (Salazar, 2013). Humanizing pedagogy focuses on the *processes* through which people actively co-construct knowledge. It stems from the scholarship and activism of Brazilian philosopher Paulo Freire and promotes a version of education in which students and teachers cooperatively examine and explore issues through critical reflection and dialogue (Salazar, 2013). In Freire's (1970) philosophy, being human is more than having a brain and body. A fully human individual thinks critically, takes control and responsibility over his or her own life, and is able to maximize his or her creative and intellectual potential. It also pushes individuals who come from different backgrounds to understand one another's differences and humanity.

Humanizing family engagement is an approach to family–school collaborations that privileges interpersonal relationships founded in mutual trust, in which educators and family members purposefully learn across their differences to pedagogically leverage a wider range of educational resources to support children's learning. It draws from research in humanizing pedagogy to envision parent involvement practices from a humanizing approach. This approach seeks to disrupt traditional paradigms of parent involvement that position minoritized families as not caring about education. As students develop and use their educational resources with caring adults across contexts of learning, this approach seeks to foster family–school engagement practices that recognize this range of knowledges, including the traditional and innovative ways in which caregivers contribute to their children's education. As I describe below, humanizing family engagement entails an examination of (1) what counts as knowledge, education, and involvement (2) ideological clarity regarding schooling, (3) teachers as learners, and (4) relationships of *confianza*/mutual trust.

What Counts. For Freire (1970, 1987) and other critical scholars, teaching and learning are viewed as political acts that are never neutral. Thus, understanding the political nature of what counts as knowledge, education, and involvement is necessary for equitable education. School walls are porous, and the power inequities outside of classrooms often seep inside. For example, how ideas are shared and taken up between a White middle-class teacher who is proficient in the English of schooling and an undocumented Mexican immigrant father who is fluent in Spanish may reflect both of their social statuses in the community and country. Such systems discount many of the knowledges, resources, and forms of engagement of minoritized parents. By recognizing the political nature of what counts as knowledge, education, and involvement, we are forced to acknowledge that to be neutral is to take a (subconscious) stance of being in support of the status quo (Bartolomé, 1994). As current academic realities illustrate, the status quo does not appear to effectively support and develop diverse students' learning. Recognizing that what is often considered knowledge, education, and involvement is socially constructed is the first step to realizing that we may be able to enact alternative possibilities.

Ideological Clarity. One of the foundational components of Freire's (1970) work is conscientization—the process of achieving critical consciousness of the world and one's place in it. If educators are going to build meaningful relationships with caregivers across differences, they need to intentionally seek out ways to foster ideological clarity regarding asymmetrical power relations, what counts as knowledge, and who counts as holding this knowledge (Bartolomé,

1994, 2004). Ideology is a set of cultural beliefs, attitudes, and values about social reality that subconsciously guide people's understandings of the world, including what counts as normal (Apple, 2004). Societies often have dominant ideologies shared by the dominant group, such as the White middle class in the United States, whose values, beliefs, and attitudes become naturalized and reinforced within large institutions such as schools (Sensoy & DiAngelo, 2012). When dominant ideologies are assumed to be absolute truths, they overlook alternative perspectives, explanations, and beliefs. They silence those who are not part of dominant societies. Unless educators develop the tools to question their own beliefs, their classroom and family engagement practices will re-create the existing dominant ideologies and silence nondominant students.

An example of a dominant ideology is the ideal of working hard as an immigrant and pulling yourself up by your bootstraps. Many White community members and educators in Marshall discussed this assumed truth in talking about immigrant students' success or challenges, often naming the ways that their own immigrant relatives several generations ago had achieved social mobility through hard work. In discussing this myth, they often interwove a second dominant ideology—that their immigrant relatives had achieved this without entering the United States illegally. Yet these two dominant ideologies elide important details. The first ignores an alternative truth that during the industrial expansion over a century ago immigrants' unskilled, low-wage labor could lead to social mobility, whereas similar unskilled low-wage labor today does not (Garcia, 2002). The second overlooks the reality that the category of "illegal immigration" did not exist in the United States prior to 1965, and thus comparing the lawfulness of previous generations of immigrants' entry into the United States to current immigration processes ignores crucial contextual differences (Chomsky, 2014). These dominant ideologies can lead to judgments that immigrants today—adults or students—simply do not work hard enough, are lazy, or are morally inferior.

In these examples, developing ideological clarity would entail learning about historical differences regarding the economy, social mobility, and U.S. immigration policies. One avenue to begin to do this would be by building trusting relationships with undocumented immigrants and learning from their perspectives and experiences. Another avenue is through teacher education. Within teacher education today, issues of difference such as undocumented status are rarely discussed. To develop ideological clarity about documentation status, teacher education would have to provide space to examine the ways U.S. immigration policies have led to an increasing association between the terms *Mexican* and *illegal immigrant* (Chomsky, 2014) and to develop tools to question such policies that dehumanize immigrants. Educators need to engage in critical examination of the stereotypes about "illegals" who "don't belong here," which are often presupposed in the media and taken up in ways that silence talk about immigration at school.

Developing ideological clarity, then, asks teachers to analyze and question their own beliefs and assumptions about the status quo so that they can "better understand if, when, and how their belief systems uncritically reflect those of the dominant society and support unfair and inequitable conditions" (Bartolomé, 2000, p. 168). Developing ideological clarity requires asking difficult questions about how we as members of the dominant group benefit from systems of privilege, even if we do not intend to, and how these systems may simultaneously devalue the resources that diverse families bring to schooling. Teachers need time, space, and guidance to develop tools to examine their own beliefs and ideologies about the political and economic hierarchies existing in the United States and how these relate to power and privilege (Bartolomé, 2004). As part of humanizing family engagement, educators are encouraged to raise their own critical consciousness to push back against the damaging xenophobic messages that can distort students' learning and obscure the breadth of resources that families bring to their children's education.

Teachers as Learners. Freire's (1970) work critiqued what he called a banking model of education, in which teachers were the holders of knowledge that they deposited to fill students' empty minds. When teachers are positioned as the sole experts on learning, the knowledges and resources that lay outside of their personal repertoire or the school-sanctioned curriculum often get silenced or overlooked. Yet, when teachers come to understand themselves as expert in some things, but also learners of others, they can open spaces for a wider range of knowledges in their classrooms. For example, most teachers at Grant Elementary knew very little about local immigration practices that led to the deportation of many students' relatives, whereas many students had tremendous expertise regarding these realities. Although all teachers at the school wanted to support their students, only those educators who created safe spaces to learn from their students were able to access these experiences and, at times, tap into them for learning.

The teacher-as-learner role is also central to reimagining family–school relationships. One of the primary stated goals of most parent involvement initiatives is to create meaningful two-way communication between educators and caregivers regarding a student's education. In practice, however, teachers often come to be viewed as the experts who fill parents' heads with information regarding schooling. This is especially true for low-income, minoritized families who are often seen as detracting from, rather than contributing to, their children's education (Cooper, 2009). Educators are often used to being experts, and it is difficult to open up the conversation. Meaningful dialogue is important as educators and caregivers engage with one another in support of a child's learning.

Confianza/*Mutual Trust.* Like other scholars who argue that caring teacher–student relationships reflective of humanizing pedagogy are essential for the academic success of minoritized students (e.g., Campano, 2007; Valenzuela, 1999), a humanizing family engagement framework assumes that students could be more academically successful if educators fostered humanizing relationships with their caregivers. *Confianza*, or mutual trust, is based on a willingness to establish personal involvement, generosity, and sharing of lives (Vélez-Ibañez, 2010). In a schooling context focused on the importance of learning across homes and schools, humanizing family engagement urges educators to consider how they can learn from and with those who are different from themselves, and provides a lens to tap the wide range of resources that families and children bring to school. In order for parents to share their perspectives and experiences with educators, especially those parents who regularly receive messages that their expertise is less important than teachers', they need to feel comfortable and confident that they will be authentically heard. In my experience with both children and parents in Marshall, I saw that without mutual trust, they often remained silent. Trust was often built by active listening as well as through teachers finding appropriate ways to share parts of themselves with students' families.

An Example of Humanizing Family Engagement

In 2009, my colleague Holly Link and I worked with a pair of 1st-grade teachers, both White, monolingual English speakers, who wanted to deepen their relationships with Mexican families. To do this, they enacted several small changes that reflected humanizing family engagement. First, they invited family members to come into their classroom to spend 30 minutes teaching something important from their lives, and several parents came in to teach soccer, share favorite stories from growing up in Mexico, and offer other educational resources. Family members engaged children through modeling, explanations, and opportunities for students to participate. Students were engaged in these lessons, and proud if their family member came in to teach. Then, teachers briefly visited the homes of those who had presented to thank them, often visiting around dinnertime and having the chance to sit with a family and share a meal, look through photo albums, or witness how siblings helped one another with homework. Finally, the teachers restrategized how to engage in mutual dialogue with immigrant caregivers during parent–teacher conferences. When these educational practices are viewed through a humanizing family engagement framework, it is clear that these educators began to engage in an alternative approach to parent involvement that helped develop supportive relationships for students' success.

These teachers expanded "what counts" by carving out time in their teaching schedules to open up spaces for Spanish-dominant family members to share their knowledges. By doing this, they ratified additional knowledges as important for all students' learning, Spanish as a language of instruction in the classroom, and immigrant parents as bearers of knowledge. They began to engage in purposeful development of "ideological clarity" by recognizing that immigrant caregivers' relative silence during conferences did not reflect indifference toward their children's education, as teachers sometimes worried. Instead, by getting to know parents and adjusting how they approached conversations in their conferences, teachers learned that many parents enacted *respeto*, or deep respect for teachers, and were nervous to question their authority related to academics. This was largely a result of cultural values from growing up in Mexico, as well as uncertainties as immigrant parents regarding how English medium schooling worked in the United States. This set of teachers also took on the role of learners by inviting families to teach and by stepping outside their comfort zones and visiting families' homes to learn from them. Families and teachers purposefully crossed into one another's home turf, which helped teachers establish relationships of mutual trust and leverage these relationships to better support students' schooling. For example, during a spring parent–teacher conference for 1st-grader Gregorio, his teacher opened by thanking his parents Julio and Lucinda for their classroom lesson and welcoming her into their home. She then asked what Gregorio tells them about school. In contrast to a relatively one-way teacher-fronted conversation during their fall conference, Gregorio's teacher and caregivers engaged in meaningful two-way dialogue in which they discussed his academic strengths and areas for growth. It took work, time, and intentionality to foster alternative family–school engagement practices, but these changes provided important pathways for teachers to authentically work with caregivers to support students' education.

Enacting Humanizing Family Engagement in an Era of Accountability

This book illustrates the potential of humanizing family engagement and pushes against the restricted versions of knowledge and learning that are prioritized in schooling today. The educational realities in this book unfolded within a context in which teachers at Grant Elementary were increasingly restricted by semi-scripted curricula and accountability-driven pedagogies. The arrival of a new superintendent in 2009 and a new principal in 2010 led to closely monitored packaged literacy and math programs as well as testing-oriented instruction. Such scripted practices left little space for the experiences and resources that children brought with them to school (Huerta, 2011). As one of the teachers, Ms. Vega, explained, "Working at a public school, your hands, legs, feet, [and] mouth are tied." The realities, opportunities, and constraints of public schooling are always in flux, and the experiences I discuss here unfolded in a particularly restrictive moment at which teachers often felt they had limited agency in how they got to know their students and families or developed their curriculum (Paris & Alim, 2014). My intent is not to deny or overlook these realities. Rather, it is to provide the space and tools needed to critically examine these realities and to create a pathway to begin talking about the ways educators come to understand the educational resources that diverse caretakers bring to their children's education.

Educators—like the students and families that they work with—are not static, two-dimensional beings. This book highlights three teachers: Ms. Vega was a superb teacher in the technical sense and tended toward more traditional approaches to parent involvement, which were foundational in her preservice training. Mrs. Drescher engaged in a more dynamic range of practices that entailed some components of humanizing family engagement. And Ms. Costanzo found ways to build meaningful relationships with students and their families to leverage their home-based knowledges for schooling. Yet this does not mean that educators are essentialized into these roles.

I hope this book provides the space to raise awareness regarding the naturalized ideologies that shape assumptions of what teaching and learning are for educators, their students, and their students' caregivers. My goal is for readers to critically examine the constraints and possibilities of adapting a humanizing approach to family engagement in their own context. In solidarity with scholars who question accountability-driven approaches to schooling, humanizing family engagement is meant as a necessary alternative to one-size-fits-all schooling and parent involvement. My aim is to present the complex educational experiences of Mexican immigrant children with their fathers and teachers as an illustration of the importance and the possibilities of humanizing family engagement.

WHAT THIS BOOK IS AND IS NOT

This book closely examines fathers' engagement in their children's educational lives to advance the goal of helping educators develop humanizing school policies and practices that create spaces to recognize and build upon students' and families' contributions to meet educational goals. This framework provides an illustration of the need for humanizing family engagement because of Latino immigrant fathers' complex politics of recognition in the United States today: Latino men are often invisible within their children's schooling and positioned as "illegal" or "criminal" in current immigration debates.

Yet this book is not meant as a "how-to" guide for working with Mexican immigrant fathers. Here, I share the experiences of fathers, students, and teachers as an illustration of a process. This process entails proactively getting to know people across many forms of difference to better understand the knowledges, experiences, and resources they bring to their children's learning. It entails personal examinations of the stereotypes and assumptions of what is often believed to be "common sense." These examinations support the critical development of ideological clarity regarding assumed truths, in order to consider alternative ways of thinking, knowing, and doing. Educators should be open to continual learning, and explorations of how a wider range of educational resources can be creatively drawn upon to reach academic goals. In each local context, this process may entail getting to know Latino fathers, or Somali caregivers, or

African American other-mothers. It entails proactively searching for ways to learn across difference. This is an invitation to try on approaches to humanizing family engagement, which intentionally seek out ways to learn from the forms of educational engagement that families bring to classrooms.

This book is organized into two parts. Part I: From Stereotypes to Humantypes and Leveraging Difference (Chapters 1–4) focuses on family–school relationships. Part II: Working with Immigrant and Undocumented Families (Chapters 5–7), focuses on the ways that a family member's undocumented status shapes children's educational experiences. In each of the following chapters, I highlight a component of the four-part framework of humanizing family engagement—purposeful development of ideological clarity; reconsidering what counts; fostering relationships of mutual trust; and reframing teachers as learners—to examine the educational experiences of fathers and their children around a central theme. I focus on individual fathers' experiences as a way to get to know humantypes and their lived complexities. Each of these cases was carefully selected to highlight in-group differences and the breadth of experiences that fathers and their children brought to living and learning in Marshall, Pennsylvania. Some of the fathers, such as Mateo, who was introduced in the opening vignette, appear in several chapters; others only appear in a single chapter or in the contextualization of the findings. Each chapter concludes with pedagogical takeaways and reflection questions in an effort to facilitate opportunities for the reader to relate the experiences of these students, parents, and teachers to his or her own life.

Each father had clear yet distinct visions of what it meant to be a father and to be engaged in his children's schooling. Although the spotlight is on fathers, these fathers' practices are situated within both parents' shared responsibilities of educating children. Chapters 2 and 3 examine the ways teachers came to understand three fathers' school and home-based engagement practices. In Chapter 2, I focus on how Julio was overlooked in terms of his son's schooling and how Ignacio's practices were misunderstood. I examine the importance of developing ideological clarity to better recognize and pedagogically leverage the educational resources that diverse students and families bring to their classrooms. In Chapter 3, I examine Mateo's relationship with his daughter's teacher, highlighting how important it is for educators to reconsider what counts as involvement. Rather than viewing families' alternative practices as signs of apathy toward their children's schooling, I show how these practices can be proactive choices that immigrant families tactically make to protect and educate their children.

Chapters 4 and 5 focus on the ways fathers develop their children's home-based literacy practices, which differed from the narrow literacy conventions prioritized in classrooms. In Chapter 4, I show how Cristián's school engagement reflected *una buena educación* (a good education), which emphasized explicit lessons and implicit modeling of how to be a linguistically appropriate bilingual speaker. His lessons about metalinguistic awareness—or knowledge about how languages work and interrelate—provided crucial tools for his daughter that helped her leverage her bilingual resources for language and literacy learning. I show that through humanizing family engagement, teachers can take on the role of learner to incorporate families' language and literacy practices into their school-based literacy instruction. In Chapter 5, I return to Mateo's pedagogies of the home to examine what counts as literacy. I focus on a story that Abi and Mateo co-narrated about police officers coming to their home as an example of the ways Mateo prepared his daughter to read both the word through her development of oracy skills and the world as a bilingual child from an undocumented family.

In Chapter 6, I present the experiences of Princess after her father was deported for a minor infraction and highlight the ways undocumented status affects elementary school students, their families, and their teachers. I illustrate both the tensions in the situation and the opportunities for teachers to foster a learning environment in which students can safely disclose their immigration experiences. Through Princess's experiences, I show how teachers deserve more support to determine ways for students to talk and write about undocumented status and schooling. In the final chapter, I invite educators to consider the obstacles and possibilities of how they can incorporate humanizing family engagement practices into their own schools and classrooms. At the close of the book, I provide a table of focal families (Appendix A) and a description of my methodology (Appendix B).

Evident in the following chapters are the educational skills, ethical values, linguistic resources, and strategic abilities that fathers instilled in their children. Through the complex educational experiences of Mexican immigrant fathers and their young children across contexts of learning, this book theorizes the need for humanizing family engagement. It centers on the promise of parent involvement practices that build upon the range of linguistic and sociocultural resources that Latin@ immigrant students and their families bring to school. It provides a window into Latino men's lives as caring fathers engaged in traditional and innovative educational practices at home, and examines the ways their children drew upon these educational resources in their elementary school classrooms. Through examples of how these resources were recognized, built upon, and overlooked in school, this book argues for the importance of humanizing family engagement as a counter-practice to the one-size-fits-all schooling that many teachers, diverse students, and families experience today.

Chapter 2

(Mis)understanding Mexican Immigrant Fathers' Parent Engagement

Julio, Lucinda, and Gregorio

Julio (29 years old) and Lucinda (30 years old) were parents of 2nd-grader Gregorio at Grant Elementary School. Julio had soft, caring eyes and a shy smile and had grown up in a rural town in Puebla, Mexico, before moving to Marshall as a teenager to join his brother. Lucinda, who filled their home with music and laughter, had grown up near the beach in Guerrero and moved to Marshall with a boyfriend in her early 20s. She and Julio met in Marshall and had two children, Gregorio (8 years old) and Lily (2 years old). Julio ran a small construction company that required long work hours, and when their second child was born, Lucinda stopped working in a local restaurant in order to stay home with their children.

Like many students from his generation in Mexico, Julio had only completed elementary school. His family of 13 children did not have enough money for him to continue his studies and, although public schooling was free in Mexico, it often required associated costs for books, uniforms, and transportation that many families could not afford. Lucinda, who had been raised by her grandparents while her own mother worked in the United States, had been able to finish high school, in part because the remittances that her mother sent helped support the costs of her continued schooling. Lucinda's more advanced studies meant she managed most of the written communication in their Pennsylvania household, including bills and school handouts. Julio, in contrast, had more developed spoken English skills from working with clients and often took the lead when communicating with monolingual English speakers. Like many couples, they relied on each other's strengths to navigate life as an immigrant family.

Ignacio, Alejandra, and Martina

Ignacio (36 years old) and Alejandra (31 years old) were the parents of 2nd-grader Martina, one of Gregorio's classmates. They grew up in economically stable families in towns near Puebla, Mexico. Ignacio had a warm smile behind his well-trimmed mustache, and his more formal clothing at school events were usually replaced by flip-flops and a backwards baseball cap at home. Ignacio and Alejandra met while living and working in Puebla and decided to move to Pennsylvania together after getting married. They came from more middle-class backgrounds compared to many other Mexican immigrant families in Marshall, such as Gregorio's, and Ignacio emphasized, "We are not rich, but middle class with work." They also had more formal schooling than most Mexican immigrant parents in Marshall. Ignacio, who never took to the rigidity of formal schooling, like many of his siblings who had professional careers in Mexico, completed *secundaria* (9th grade), whereas Alejandra completed a technical career in *preparatoria* (12th grade). In a country where less than a quarter of students continue on to higher education, their level of education was significant. Both Ignacio and Alejandra also had high levels of Spanish literacy, strong technological know-how, and were attuned to pedagogical approaches in general.

Yet, as undocumented immigrants, their employment opportunities and income differed little from those of other Mexican immigrants who came from more humble resources and limited opportunities for formal education. Alejandra worked in local restaurants and cleaning homes, and Ignacio worked in manual labor in sectors such as roofing. Although among fellow Mexican immigrants Ignacio and Alejandra's class backgrounds were apparent, such differences were invisible to their White and Black counterparts in Marshall. At Grant Elementary, most educators assumed that Mexican immigrant parents almost unilaterally came from rural backgrounds, poverty, and limited formal schooling. This was illustrated during pickup one day when the guidance counselor was giving away donated food, and asked me to approach a family from Mexico because she did not speak Spanish. I had met this family before and knew that they were well educated, came from an urban area, and earned a stable income in Marshall. Insinuating that they needed donated food would come across as insulting, and although I tried to push back, the counselor insisted. The family was indeed insulted. On other occasions, teachers questioned the utility of sending home school handouts in Spanish, as they believed many parents were unable to read in either English or Spanish. Although I occasionally met a parent who had not had the opportunity to develop basic literacy, this was extremely rare. I encouraged educators to consider how the handouts translated into technical Spanish may be difficult for parents to understand, how the Spanish translations were not always accurate or reflective of the varieties of Spanish spoken by parents, and how U.S-specific contextual knowledge of schooling was often needed to understand many of the handouts. Because most teachers could not easily discern caregivers' literacy skills in Spanish, they often relied upon things they had heard that were not based in families' actual abilities (see Gallo, Link, Allard, Wortham, & Mortimer, 2014).

In this chapter, I draw on Julio's and Ignacio's experiences with their children's teacher to show how narrow, traditional approaches to parent involvement cause educators to overlook or negatively evaluate diverse caretakers' engagement practices. Julio's case illustrates the ways that most Mexican immigrant fathers tended to be overlooked in school, and how the subtle messages fathers received about their role silenced their visible contributions and closed down opportunities for educators to learn how these fathers were engaged in their children's educational lives. Ignacio, in contrast, was not overlooked. Instead, he was misunderstood. I show how his relatively traditional engagement practices, when performed by a Spanish-dominant Mexican immigrant man, were evaluated as detrimental to his daughter's academic growth. Central to this chapter are the gendered expectations that subtly and overtly shape the opportunities that fathers are given to be seen as involved in their children's schooling, and how explicitly questioning these gendered expectations can open up opportunities to better understand fathers' educational engagement. In the discussion, I focus on the importance of ideological clarity so that educators can seek out ways to develop a critical awareness of whom and what they notice in terms of family school engagement.

GREGORIO AND MARTINA ACROSS HOME AND SCHOOL CONTEXTS

Julio and Lucinda's son Gregorio, whom they often called Greggy, was born in Marshall. He was a slender and athletic 2nd-grader with wire-rimmed glasses who loved to draw. He bubbled with energy—so much so that his parents constantly searched for activities that would tire him out. He was much more comfortable expressing himself in English than Spanish: Since infancy, he had attended English medium day care and then preschool. During his first 2 years of elementary school, he was positioned as a model student with optimal grades, but in 2nd grade he began to struggle in reading and writing. He had a curious mind, always wanting to learn more about how things worked or to share personal connections to a given topic. After school, he attended a homework help program at the local bilingual service agency, played with friends in the neighborhood from a mix of ethnic backgrounds, or played with his baby sister. His parents appreciated Greggy's many talents, although they often wished he valued the many educational and material resources he was afforded in Pennsylvania that had never been a part of their lives in Mexico.

Ignacio and Alejandra's only child, Martina (8 years old), was a classmate of Gregorio's who was also born in Marshall. Alejandra sometimes thought about having a second child, but Ignacio worried that with more children he would not be able to fully dedicate himself to each one. He had grown up as one of eight children in Mexico and did not want to be like his own father, whom he saw as being too busy to pay attention to his kids. Martina's family lived in a multilevel rowhouse that they shared with some of Alejandra's male relatives. In part because of a work-related injury several years earlier, Ignacio was Martina's primary caretaker during out-of-school hours. Although he and Alejandra alternated nights in which they helped Martina with her homework, his more developed English and math skills often resulted in his leading role with schoolwork. His engagement practices were largely reflective of desirable middle-class practices in U.S. schools, although they were not understood this way by teachers. Instead, he was seen as being overbearing and causing educational challenges for his daughter.

Martina was a goofy and sentimental 2nd-grader who exhibited kindness as well as an affinity for benign practical jokes. Unlike most children from immigrant families in Marshall, she had her own bedroom, which her father had painted with her favorite hues of purple. He hung her pop star Hannah Montana posters and meticulously lined the ceiling with glow-in-the-dark stars so she could *"ver el cielo"* (see the sky) as she slept. Martina had attended a half-day bilingual preschool, the only one in Marshall, that was part of a family literacy program. Martina's preschool was designed to prepare children for English medium kindergarten, as there were no bilingual elementary schools in the district. By the time she enrolled in kindergarten, like many children from Spanish-dominant households who attended preschool, her development of school-based English meant that she was not placed in English as a Second Language (ESL) classes.

Outside of school, Martina would giggle uncontrollably with her friends or parents and engaged in an array of educational activities. In her free time, she loved to go swimming with her parents, play on the computer with her dad, attend the violin classes her father had enrolled her in, and communicate with her relatives in Mexico, whom she had recently met for the first time. Like many parents who did not have "papers," or documentation, to reside in the United States, Ignacio and Alejandra could not go with her on this meaningful family trip to Mexico. Unlike Martina, who was a U.S.-born citizen, as immigrants without documents they could not recross the border with ease. Ignacio highlighted the difficulty of navigating conversations of documentation status with his daughter: "Sometimes we don't even know what to tell her. We tell her, it's not that 'We don't have papers.' We say, 'We weren't born here.'" Martina's teacher was Ms. Vega, and like most teachers at Grant Elementary, she was not aware of how documentation status affected families in these ways.

Ms. Vega, Gregorio and Martina's 2nd-grade teacher, grew up in wealthier suburbs outside of Marshall and had been working at Grant since she had graduated from college 3 years earlier. Her father was an upper-class immigrant from South America who had come to Pennsylvania for boarding school and then college. While studying, he met her mother, who was White (non-Latina) and from Pennsylvania. As a relatively new teacher, Ms. Vega was consumed with lesson planning and execution, especially as the curriculum kept changing throughout the year as a result of administrative changes. She would often arrive at school at 6:00 A.M. to plan for the day. Her lessons stuck closely to the curriculum and her class rarely strayed from the paced schedule. She spoke English with a Pennsylvania accent, and though she could understand a fair amount of Spanish, she spoke little. Families rarely realized she had Latina heritage, and when I explained that Ms. Vega understood much of what we said in Spanish, parents responded with surprise.

Ms. Vega was kind to families and dedicated to supporting her students' academic success, yet she intentionally avoided personal topics with students and overall knew little about the day-to-day realities in many of her students' lives. Her philosophy was that children who entered her classroom would enter what she called a "safe zone," a space in which they did not have to think about the challenges they may be facing outside of school. She thought it best not to bring attention to experiences of difference in her classroom, as she worried that students would adopt a mentality that she described as "I don't wanna play with him. Something's different." Thus, she thought it was safest to avoid discussions of difference. As a newer, untenured teacher with limited protections from losing her position, she was also fearful of how she could be held legally responsible for broaching difficult topics. She explained, "when in doubt these days, you [the teacher] are at fault." Her pedagogical approach—developed through her extensive preservice and graduate training—prioritized teaching as a relatively depersonalized implementation of methods and techniques to support students' academic success. Such an approach aligned with the assessment-based focus of schooling in 2010 in which teachers felt increasing pressures to meet adequate yearly progress and state benchmarks. Yet this approach left limited spaces for humanizing pedagogies, which recognize and build upon the range of knowledges that students and families from diverse backgrounds bring to schooling.

In Ms. Vega's classroom of 21 students, Martina and Gregorio were two of 13 Latin@ immigrant students, most of whom were born in Marshall or other parts of the United States to Mexican immigrant parents. Their remaining classmates were African American (6), White (1), and of White and Mexican heritage (1). Her classroom was bright and cheerful, with student writing, number lines, and other educational materials lining the walls. Their shared tables formed a U that faced a SMART Board. Whole-group teacher-fronted lessons were short presentations of the newly adopted literacy, math, social studies, or science curricula, often with technology-based supports. Brief mini-lessons related to literacy activities were also conducted in the large carpeted area lined with the class library. Much of their day was dedicated to carefully orchestrated learning centers, ranging from math activities, guided reading, readers' theater, computer-mediated learning programs, and science activities. Their classroom was often buzzing with activity, as students worked in pairs or small groups, carefully guided by Ms. Vega. In a typical student-directed math center, it was common to hear Martina reach out to help a classmate and ask things like "You can't do it? *Mira.* (Look). This is five. So use five. Okay?" During whole-group instruction,

Gregorio would often multitask, such as reading a book hidden beneath his desk, which gave the impression that he was not paying attention. Gregorio had great enthusiasm for learning and parents who sought out supports for his educational development, but because of his high energy, in 2nd grade he began to face some academic challenges. And despite Martina's excellent behavior, her focus in school, and her parents' intensive efforts to support her academically, she struggled in many subject areas.

MODELS OF PARENT INVOLVEMENT

Overall, the expected family engagement practices at Grant Elementary were similar to those from a traditional model. *Traditional parent involvement* models tend to prevail in U.S. schools, and offer relatively restrictive possibilities for what can count as knowledge, education, and involvement. For many teachers, they seem like "common sense," as they often align with most teachers' own upbringings as part of the U.S. middle class. In traditional approaches, there is no pathway for teachers to develop ideological clarity or tools to analyze their own beliefs and assumptions about what are normal and desirable parent involvement practices. Traditional approaches assume that parents from all backgrounds are responsible for assisting educators with their children's integration into mainstream schooling. This assistance often includes parents' help with school-sanctioned tasks (homework), attendance at school events, and volunteering for the school. As reflected in Joyce Epstein's (2010) overlapping spheres model, the aim is to create consistency between homes and schools. As Stuart Greene (2013) highlights, Epstein's model does not account for the power differentials between predominantly White middle-class teachers and low-income parents of color. In practice, this model often leads to parent involvement practices that emphasize parents' obligations to schools rather than teachers' mutual responsibilities to families. In traditional models, parents are expected to learn teachers' approaches to schooling, whereas teachers are not expected to reciprocate. This has resulted in a push toward "school-like" families in which parents take on a teacher-like role within the home environment and shape home-based interactions to mirror school routines.

Parents, especially those from minoritized backgrounds, who do not eagerly engage in these types of practices in recognizable ways are often positioned by educators as not caring about their children's education. As Fabienne Doucet (2011a) argues, schools have the power in determining what counts as parent involvement, and parents who are under-, over-, or differently involved are often negatively positioned by educators. As the case of Ignacio illustrates, caregivers of color who engage in relatively desirable parent involvement practices by traditional standards can still be perceived by teachers as being involved in the wrong kind of ways. Although educators who operate from traditional approaches rarely intend to stifle meaningful communication, family–school communication from this approach tends to be unidirectional. Like Freire's critique (1970) of the banking model of education, in these approaches teachers are experts who tell parents about desirable school practices. They often focus on mothers as the recipients of this information, and value only a narrow frame of linguistic and educational resources.

FAMILY–SCHOOL ENGAGEMENT AT GRANT ELEMENTARY

Overview of Practices

Grant Elementary worked with approximately 400 African American and Latin@ immigrant students. Grant teachers were primarily younger, White, middle-class women who only spoke English and lived in wealthier suburbs. Teachers at Grant believed that "parent involvement" mattered and that they could differentiate between involved and uninvolved parents. For example, Ms. Vega explained the importance of parent involvement in the following way: "If the parents are involved in the kids' homework and have interest in what the kids are doing at school, it shows because the kids are more invested in it, interested in it at school." Another teacher, Mrs. Drescher, emphasized that even if parents could not attend school events, she could tell when they were involved at home "because the children care more . . . about learning." She felt she could tell through her daily interactions with her students, such as signed papers being returned to the school, students talking about reading at home, and the emphasis that she felt Latin@ parents placed on good behavior. Mrs. Cieza, the ESL teacher, emphasized how she believed students with involved parents might not always be the most academically advanced students, but they were the ones with the strongest connections to schooling. Overall, at Grant Elementary, parents were expected to:

- help with homework,
- respond to frequent handouts,
- be accessible by phone in case a problem arose;
- attend school-based events such as parent–teacher conferences, and
- show they "cared" about their children's schooling.

It is important to note that within this particular school, Mexican immigrant families were sometimes talked about as a "model minority" compared with African American families, but not in ways that authentically valued the educational resources that Mexican families brought to their children's schooling. While reflecting upon the student groups she had worked with at Grant, during an interview one teacher stressed that she "like[d] the transition that the population has taken." When asked to elaborate, she explained, "Our Latino families on the whole are intact, caring, working, [have a good] work ethic, [and] care about education, whereas we really had a lot of missing parents with our other population, not caring as much." Such comments were problematic, and illustrate how African American families were understood through traditional involvement lenses in which teachers had limited opportunities to foster interpersonal relationships or question the ideologies that shaped their perceptions. Yet, although teachers spoke fondly about newcomers from Mexico and their values, they engaged in what Sofia Villenas (2002) terms *benevolent racism*: Although they were well intentioned, they often viewed families' academic resources through deficit lenses, such as believing these families did not know English or were not engaging in mainstream literacy practices. Many educators also engaged in aspects of soft care (Valenzuela, 1999), in which they felt affinity for Latin@ families and students, but also pitied their circumstances and at times did not hold them to high academic expectations (see Link, Gallo, & Wortham, in press). Although Grant teachers' welcoming attitudes toward Latin@ families may have opened up opportunities to begin to engage in humanizing engagement, there were additional opportunities for teachers to better understand and build upon the familial educational resources that all their students brought to schooling. And fathers, including Mexican immigrant fathers, tended to be overlooked in terms of their family engagement practices.

Family–School Engagement as Mothers' Work: Fathers' Invisibility

Teachers' routine practices both at school and during family–school events illustrate the ways in which family–school engagement was often understood as the mother's role. One way teachers prioritized mothers was in student-based interactions during the school day. For example, teachers would often say, "Take this home. Give it to your *mom*!" or "So if you went home to talk to your mom today about the story that we read, you'd tell your mom. . . ." This occurred in subtle yet consistent ways during school events as well. Teachers tended to only name a child's mother, even when both parents arrived. One afternoon, Ms. Vega repeatedly mentioned "Martina's mom" coming in to meet, although Martina's father, Ignacio, had also attended every school event that year. As Martina's parents walked up the stairs and waved hello, Ms. Vega commented, "Oh, Martina's mom is here," failing to mention Ignacio, who offered a warm smile as he approached. Subconscious and subtle interactions such as this one are innocent, yet they are persistent reminders of how family engagement in schools is often understood as mothers' work, which overlooks fathers' engagement in their children's schooling.

During face-to-face interactions, teachers also tended to orient more toward mothers if both parents were present: In conferences, they would place documents on the table in front of mothers, orient their eye gaze toward mothers, build upon mothers' contributions more than fathers', and occasionally attribute fathers' contributions to mothers. For example, Mrs. Drescher met with one boy's father during fall conferences where they discussed the boy's tendency to be distracted. During the spring conference, which both parents attended, Mrs. Drescher referenced this earlier conversation, explicitly naming that she had had it with "mom." The boy's parents did not correct her, perhaps out of a desire to respect the teacher's authority. Even when Mexican immigrant fathers were actively participating in traditional school-based events in traditional ways, mothers tended to be credited for their family's engagement.

At Grant, very well-intentioned and welcoming teachers tended to mention, notice, and engage with mothers more than fathers. In general, fathers from any racial or ethnic background were rarely recognized or talked about, even when they were physically present in schools and engaged in relatively mainstream engagement practices. At Grant and across the United States, *who* counts as engaged and *what* counts as engagement are shaped by factors such as gender, race, nationality, language, and immigration status. In this chapter, I focus on Julio, who was overlooked, and Ignacio, who was misunderstood.

JULIO'S OVERLOOKED ENGAGEMENT

Greggy's father, Julio, worked long hours running a construction company and his wife, Lucinda, stayed home to care for their two young children. In terms of assisting with more traditional family–school engagement practices, Julio lacked the time and confidence to help with homework or reading. Lucinda took on these responsibilities because she was regularly at home and had more formal schooling. Yet Julio emphasized that he wanted to know how Greggy was doing in school, and he tried to attend school events to learn about his son's progress. He explained, "I'm not helping him all the time, but it does interest me to know how he's doing in school. Not just the mom." When reflecting upon the ways Mexican fathers were often talked about in terms of family–school relationships, he lamented, "No one has really paid attention to this. . . . Everyone's focused on moms."

There were many ways Julio was engaged in supporting Gregorio's education. These included knowing the details of his son's daily schooling practices, verbalizing high expectations regarding Greggy's educational attainment, providing real-world exposure to his own difficult work experiences to motivate Greggy to excel academically, and engaging in collaborative play. He had close relationships with his children and sought out creative ways to be present in their lives, even when he could not physically be with them. He would speak to his children multiple times a day on the phone and always tried to figure out what types of activities would be of interest to Gregorio to foster his development. On weekends, Julio largely engaged in creative play with his children, such as playfully reenacting boxing matches, organizing dart competitions, and completing puzzles. He regularly spoke to Gregorio about the importance of excelling in school and going on to college so that he would not end up with a labor-intensive job like Julio's. In an interview Julio explained:

> I want him [Gregorio] to keep on studying because I don't want him to work like I do. I tell him that I don't want him to have a job like mine where you start at six in the morning and don't get home until nine at night . . . and sometimes I take him to work with me so that that he sees that it's not that easy and ask him, "Do you want to work like this?" so that he'll say, "No, instead of being here I'm going to work hard at school." . . . And one day he'll graduate, and he'll be someone, and he won't have to go around to see if there is manual labor available.

Julio and Lucinda desired a better future for their children and made great sacrifices so they could access educational opportunities in the United States. These sacrifices included working long hours in manual labor (for Julio) and not being able to see family in Mexico because their undocumented status meant they could not safely cross the border. When Lucinda's grandmother, who had raised her, passed away in Mexico, the pain of not being able to return to say good-bye was excruciating. Living in the United States as an undocumented immigrant came with the sacrifice of not being able to see family members in Mexico, including saying good-bye to loved ones at the end of their lives.

One of the primary reasons Gregorio's family lived in the United States was to provide promising educational futures for their U.S.-born children. Education was at the core of their familial migration decisions, and both parents regularly attended parent–teacher conferences to understand Greggy's academic progress. During his fall conference in 2nd grade, Julio and Lucinda sat across the table from Ms. Vega, and I served as the interpreter.[1] She began the conference by placing the sign-in sheet, pen, and report card in front of Lucinda, implicitly sending the message that Gregorio's mother was the one responsible for schooling. During an informal interview with me, Julio reflected how this happened during doctor's appointments as well: The individuals in charge tended to speak with Lucinda, as if he were not even there. For the first 9 minutes of the conference, Ms. Vega shared updates on Gregorio's progress, highlighting her concerns about his writing as well as his reading, which was assessed as 1 year below grade level. Ms. Vega's body language was fully oriented toward Lucinda, and throughout these explanations, she never visibly looked in Julio's direction. If she had, she would have seen that he was intently looking at her and was visibly concerned, his brow deeply furrowed and his eyes wide with shock due to Greggy's academic struggles. Lucinda, who was able to make eye contact with Ms. Vega throughout the conference, occasionally asked questions about Gregorio's writing, which Ms. Vega addressed. At the end of the conference, Julio, shaking his head, tried to contribute his perspective:

> *Julio:* Um-hm. *No está bien.* (It's not okay.)
> *Interpreter:* It's not okay—
> *Julio:* No.
> *Ms. Vega:* So I think these could be higher if he listened and if he was a little more focused in class, I could see his reading improving especially. . . .

Although Ms. Vega had responded to several of Lucinda's inquiries regarding writing earlier in the conference, she did not respond to Julio's concerns. Instead, she continued with her next point. This was not an intentional move by Ms. Vega, but it left Julio and Lucinda feeling frustrated and highly concerned about their son's educational future. It also left Julio feeling like his perspectives did not matter.

After the conference, Julio commented, "I didn't like the conference at all." He explained that he had wanted to say more during the conference, to push Ms. Vega more regarding the ways Gregorio's writing development was being supported in school: "I wanted to tell her that, but I didn't say anything." In the pressure of the conference, he kept his thoughts to himself, and without intentional moves on the part of the educator to invite his perspectives, they were silenced. Because Julio spoke little during the conference, his silence could have given the impression that he was not interested in his son's education. Yet this could not have been further from the truth. After this conference, Julio pessimistically shared, "Ahh. I don't know what we're doing here [in the United States] if we're doing it for our kids and they don't study . . . it's better that we go to Mexico—what are we doing here if, as the teacher said, Greggy's doing poorly?" Ultimately, the family did not relocate to Mexico, but their concerns about Gregorio's schooling continued.

As Julio's experiences illustrate, the depersonalized sharing of a child's academic progress leaves minoritized parents feeling that their perspectives are unwelcome. Many fathers receive clear signals that conversations about their child's schooling are not geared toward them. This occurs through educators' body language, how fathers' comments are not seriously taken up, and how materials are not placed in front of them. This sends messages that their contributions are not important and perpetuates fathers' relative silence during school events. These messages are not intentional—they are subtle aspects of interactions that accumulate into silencing. When fathers do not share their experiences and perspectives, teachers are not able to learn about the ways in which fathers are engaged in their children's learning and thus, are likely to overlook them.

Next, I focus on the experiences of Ignacio, who was not overlooked in terms of his engagement in his daughter's schooling. Yet, instead of understanding his educational practices as supporting his daughter, teachers misunderstood his efforts as detracting from her educational success. Together, the cases of these two fathers illustrate how breaking the cycle of gendered assumptions about parent involvement, which often result in overlooking or misunderstanding fathers, requires developing ideological clarity and making intentional moves to learn from and with diverse caregivers.

IGNACIO'S MISUNDERSTOOD ENGAGEMENT

As shown above, parent–teacher conferences were often stressful for parents, yet they were stressful for teachers at Grant Elementary as well. Like many teachers, Ms. Vega was nervous about explaining all the standards and goals covered in her classroom during the 15 minutes allotted for each conference. She was unsure how she would cover everything in both languages without additional time and felt a bit awkward when speaking to families via an interpreter. Although schools in the district were required to provide interpreters for family communication, the tight budget left limited funds to hire professionals. In addition, as a newly established Latin@ immigrant community, there were few bilingual adults to provide their support, and Marshall had to rely on volunteers from local universities and religious organizations, who varied in their experience as interpreters.

Administrators regularly talked about "improving parent involvement," and Ms. Vega knew that family attendance at conferences was a measure to assess the quality of their elementary school. Yet there were never opportunities to decide what "improving parent involvement" meant, or how time in conferences could be best leveraged to meet these goals with families. In an interview the day following conferences, Ms. Vega reflected upon how no one in her preservice or inservice training covered what her conferences should entail or how to work with an interpreter effectively. To run her conferences, she relied on the official documents—filled with pedagogical jargon from the statewide assessments—that were distributed to parents about the 2nd-grade curriculum and standards. One such document was a poster that included (in English) every learning standard they would cover that year, with links to online resources. She commented right before conferences that she thought it would be overwhelming for most families. Nonetheless, her understanding was that she was supposed to give it to families, so she added this to the pile of documents to cover. Even though she often felt frustrated at the end of her 2-day conference marathon and told herself she would do things differently next time, these intentions quickly moved to the back of her mind as she took on the day-to-day demands of teaching. Although "improving parent involvement" was named as a priority in the district, as teachers they were given limited time or resources to examine what this meant, or how to achieve it.

Ignacio's Previous Engagement Experiences

At home, Martina's father, Ignacio, often had the type of smile that made the edges of his eyes crinkle in delight. He could sometimes be serious, and he was also caring and fun-loving with his daughter. When asked about her favorite memory with her father, Martina broke down into tears of happiness and explained several times, "He's always there for me." It was typical to see their feet dangling off the side of the bed as they worked through math problems together, Ignacio teaching her new jump-rope tricks, or him crouched down next to the computer as he taught her how to navigate online resources. This side of Ignacio, however, was not visible in his school-based interactions. Because of a previous incident during a school fieldtrip, he was uncomfortable within the school building, which contributed to him sometimes appearing anxious.

In the spring of Martina's kindergarten year, Ignacio participated in the traditional parent engagement practice of chaperoning a fieldtrip to a local farm. Several years earlier, Ignacio had fallen from a roof while working under dangerous conditions, a common reality in many of the jobs available to Latin@ immigrants. The accident had required many surgeries and a lengthy recovery. It also resulted in a long-term injury that left his arm scarred and prevented him from working or lifting heavy objects. Unlike the way teachers often attempted to engage Mexican immigrant mothers in small talk when they chaperoned, such as asking Martina's mother Alejandra the names of plants and their uses in Mexico during an outing to an arboretum, during this fieldtrip, teachers made no visible efforts to communicate with Ignacio, except to ask him and another Mexican father to move heavy boxes of school lunches off the bus. This was an example of how men were widely overlooked in schools, except when they could be used for physical labor.

In an interview several years later, Ignacio and Alejandra reflected upon how that incident, combined with the uncensored attention that Ignacio received from children if they saw the scars on his arm, made him uncomfortable at school. When I mentioned Ignacio being asked to move the lunches during the kindergarten fieldtrip, Alejandra jumped in to explain: "And that's why he doesn't want to go on the fieldtrips. . . . He talked to me about it and he said, 'Look, this happened,'" so he stopped going. This incident, which had occurred 2 years before this conversation remained fresh in their minds, and had played a pivotal role in how Ignacio engaged in school-based engagement practices. Ignacio further explained, "Sometimes I can't hide it [my arm], either. You can see it . . . and the kids ask me, 'Ay, what happened to you?' I say, 'My wife hit me' and I try to get out of it by joking around because it is hard to explain it to kids." During conferences, Ignacio was often bundled in several long-sleeved shirts, sometimes awkwardly wearing a coat on just the side with his injured arm to hide the scarring. He explained, "Sometimes I wear a sweater or something, because otherwise people can see it." His serious expression at school events was exacerbated by his overall discomfort in school, which he attributed to unwanted attention related to his scarred arm and the traumatizing incident during the kindergarten fieldtrip. Yet Ignacio still attended every single family event held at the school, including some without Alejandra, such as parent training for student literacy development.

Ignacio's Engagement in 2nd Grade

The first time Ms. Vega recalled having met Ignacio was during parent–teacher conferences in the fall. During this particular fall conference, Ignacio was initially smiling and friendly. Similar to the flow of her conference with Gregorio's parents, Ms. Vega began the conference by asking Ignacio and Alejandra to sign in and directing her comments, eye gaze, and placement of documents to Alejandra or the interpreter (Sarah), rather than to both parents. Similar to Gregorio's conference, this highlights how traditional approaches to parent involvement often prioritize mothers over fathers. As in traditional approaches to family involvement in which the teacher shares her expertise with parents rather than engaging in dialogue with them, Ms. Vega then spent the first 15 minutes, without pause, covering her talking points related to 2nd grade. As I have shown through my analyses of conferences with Kathryn Howard (Howard & Lipinoga, 2010), like most teachers Ms. Vega drew upon authoritative school documents, such as five-page report cards, to guide and support her explanations. This had the effect of silencing parents' contributions. The technical language related to early literacy development and state standardized testing was difficult for parents to understand, even when translated in Spanish.

By subconsciously taking on traditional approaches in which the teacher is the primary expert, Ms. Vega did not create a space for Martina's parents to share the ways they were engaged in supporting her schooling. This sent the implicit message that their involvement practices were unimportant or deficient. Ignacio's body language shifted dramatically during the first minutes of the conference when Ms. Vega shared the reading spectrum in which Martina had scored at a kindergarten rather than a 2nd-grade level. His smile gave way to a furrowed brow, and he spent the rest of the conference alternating among resting his face on his palm, tightly crossing his arms over his chest, and fidgeting. Alejandra also took on a serious demeanor throughout the conference, but broke into nervous smiles when she caught the teacher's eye, something that was possible because the teacher primarily looked toward her. During her opening talk, Ms. Vega also shared, emphatically, that Ignacio and Alejandra needed to read with Martina every night. This was something that—unbeknownst to Ms. Vega—Ignacio and Alejandra were already doing. They were parents who carefully crafted their schedules to maximize educational opportunities for their daughter and who proactively sought out resources to support their daughter's literacy development. An insinuation that they were not reading with Martina came across as insulting and framed Martina's educational challenges as at least partially her parents' fault.

Ms. Vega provided the first opportunity for Martina's parents to speak by asking if there were "any other questions," 15 minutes after she started talking. Unlike Julio, who had decided to keep his thoughts to himself, Ignacio gave a nervous smile, said, "*muchas preguntas*" (many questions), and then went into a long explanation of the things they had noticed at home with Martina's learning and their concerns about how, through school and home, they could better support Martina's academic development:

> *Ignacio:* So, does she [Martina] have problems? Because if she truly has problems . . . if she is not developing—I mean, what is the age that she should be able to add 30 plus 5?
>
> (Sarah, as the interpreter, checks that Ms. Vega understood Ignacio's points in Spanish, which Ms. Vega confirms. Sarah then explains to Ignacio and Alejandra that Ms. Vega can understand a fair amount of Spanish because her father spoke Spanish, which surprises Martina's parents.)
>
> *Ms. Vega:* Sometimes it does take her—she's a little slower to think about it. But that's okay at this stage. As long as they're using strategies at all to get the answer, it will become more automatic. She is pretty much on level in math. . . . Keep practicing, more math workbooks from the dollar store, just drill and practice. And just have her read to you every night. . . .
> *Ignacio:* Our system [in Mexico] is different. If we were like this, at this level—
> *Alejandra:* She wouldn't pass. She wouldn't pass.
> *Ignacio:* She'd repeat the year.

Ms. Vega, aligning to a traditional framework in which student improvement occurred through school-like routines at home, suggested that Martina get more practice and that more encouragement would help Martina, as she sometimes seemed unsure of herself.

As is evident in his comments about "our system is different," Ignacio regularly compared Grant Elementary to the pedagogical approaches he had experienced in Mexico. He mentioned Martina's report card grade of two out of four, which in Marshall indicated scoring from the statewide assessment of "approaching competency" in the desired skill, and was a nonalarming grade for students. In Mexico, however, two out of four (a 50% score, in Ignacio's mind), would be considered failing and, because of grade promotion practices, would mean Martina would have to repeat the entire school year. Here and throughout his meetings with Ms. Vega, Ignacio could clearly articulate the routines from his upbringing in Mexico that formed his understanding of schooling practices, and recognized that they were different from those in Marshall. He explained to Ms. Vega, "Even though we did not study in this country, we did study in another country; we did study, but it was different." Ignacio and Alejandra were middle-class parents and felt confident displaying their pedagogical knowledge while seeking out ways to work with Ms. Vega. Most other immigrant parents at Grant Elementary did not do this. Yet, as an immigrant parent who was experiencing U.S. schools for the first time through his daughter, Ignacio did not have a clear understanding of local educational practices. These included things such as an outlook of positive reinforcement that focused on verbalizing what kids did well so that they would continue to do it or the grading system modeled after statewide assessments. Ms. Vega, in contrast, operated from a traditional approach. She had not been given the time, space, or supports to critically examine what counted as involvement and seemed relatively unaware of the specificity of the routines within the schooling system. As a new teacher, these were also the only practices she had ever known, reducing opportunities for her to critically reflect upon their nonuniversality.

Ignacio's engagement practices should have mapped onto desirable practices at Grant Elementary, but his practices were instead seen as detracting from his daughter's learning. In a calm voice, Ignacio diplomatically shared his frustrations that he and Alejandra had been hearing the same thing about Martina's learning from teachers for 3 years and he wanted to figure out if Martina simply learned at a different pace or if she had legitimate learning difficulties that required attention. Reflecting what would be considered expected middle-class parent involvement practices in the United States, he advocated for his daughter and put pressure on the school to help determine the issues, while simultaneously offering to help in any way possible. He emphasized that he was not blaming Ms. Vega, sharing during the conference, "I am not saying that she [Ms. Vega] is to blame, but rather that we are trying to figure out a way to help Martina." Yet his concerns and advocacy, conducted by a Mexican immigrant father in Spanish rather than a White middle-class parent in English, were taken up by the teacher as overbearing rather than supportive. After the conference, Ms. Vega shared in an interview that the only father who really stood out to her in terms of involvement was Ignacio, but that she worried he was too critical of Martina and that this may impede her academic development.

Three months later, Ms. Vega met with Ignacio and Alejandra again as a special follow-up regarding Martina's progress. During the fall conference, Alejandra had suggested this follow-up, saying, "I was wondering if she [Ms. Vega] would give us a time to meet again so that we can see how Martina is advancing. Just as much for us as well as her [Martina's] improvement at school. This way, we'll also see ourselves as obliged to help Martina a little bit more." As part of a plan to provide more support for Martina's English literacy development, Ms. Vega had also started sending home a purple folder with extra literacy practice for Martina. Her directions, however, were not clear to Martina's parents, and they thought they were supposed to finish it all at once. Ms. Vega often relied on Martina to relay information through oral instructions to her parents, which Martina could not easily explain in Spanish. By 2nd grade, Martina was English dominant in ways that were appropriate for her age and grade level, as a student who had attended English-only schooling for 3 years. And although Ignacio had moderately developed English language and literacy skills, there were many school-specific assignments and routines that he could not understand. This led to confusion regarding how much additional work Martina was supposed to complete each night. Martina had also started an after-school literacy program, which kept her busy until 5:30 P.M.

Ignacio and Alejandra believed that the contents of the purple folder, in addition to Martina's regular homework and after-school program, were too much, but they felt they should comply with the teacher's request. Interestingly, Ms. Vega also felt Martina's parents put too much pressure on her and wanted her to do too much, but she thought they wanted Martina to keep doing the additional practice, so she kept sending it home. Although everyone involved was searching for ways to support Martina, they had not developed a trusting relationship for effective two-way communication to learn from one another and effectively support her learning.

The second meeting brought to light a misalignment on how to better support Martina's writing development. Writing development at Grant Elementary focused on creative stories, flexibility with invented spelling, writing for various purposes, and the inclusion of details. From their upbringings in Mexico, Ignacio and Alejandra viewed writing development as something learned through accurately copying texts, with emphasis also placed on handwriting. During the meeting, Ignacio provided insight into Martina's home-based literacy interests, such as her love of copying lyrics to songs. This literacy practice met the expectations of writing in Mexico, but did not align with the versions of writing valued at Grant Elementary. Neither Ms. Vega nor Martina's parents appeared to understand that they were enacting different concepts of writing, and that Ms. Vega's advice to engage in more writing at home might not help Martina develop the tools that the school curriculum demanded.

By the end of the meeting, Ms. Vega noticed that Alejandra and, especially, Ignacio were visibly frustrated. She began sharing her concerns during informal interviews with me that Martina needed more encouragement and that her father appeared very serious and overbearing. Her understanding of Martina's participation in school presupposed parents who were not encouraging and placed too much pressure on Martina. When discussing Martina's writing during an interview, Ms. Vega explained, "I kind of have this feeling that—I don't know if her work at home is a little bit too, I don't know, if the parents are—because I see that she's a little bit too much a perfectionist, especially in writing where she's so much focused on trying to get it right that she'll write one sentence in an hour." She then went on to emphasize, unsolicited, "He [Ignacio] can seem very disappointed easily in Martina. And I don't know if that's really gonna bring forth the kind of follow-through that he wants to see. I think if he's a little more positive, it might be better." Martina's parents, and Ignacio in particular, were seen as engaged in Martina's schooling, but not in ways that were understood as helpful to her academic growth.

ENVISIONING HUMANIZING FAMILY ENGAGEMENT:
IDEOLOGICAL CLARITY

Through the experiences of Julio and Ignacio, I have shown how traditional approaches to family–school relationships caused a well-intentioned educator to overlook and misunderstand fathers' engagement practices. Returning to the first key feature of humanizing family engagement, the development of ideological clarity, this next section discusses how a humanizing approach could provide a pathway to better support schooling for students like Gregorio and Martina.

Ideological Clarity: Julio

Differences such as gender, nationality, language, and documentation status play a subconscious role in how caregivers' educational contributions are understood and valued. Julio, like most fathers at Grant Elementary, was not treated as a contributor to his son's schooling. This unfolded in subtle, rather than explicit, ways. He picked up on signals that his contributions were less important than his wife's and held back his questions and perspectives. His silence during school-based events contributed to a cycle in which he was overlooked. He did not feel welcome to contribute, and as he and Ms. Vega never engaged in authentic dialogue about Gregorio's schooling, she never had the chance to learn about the important ways in which he supported his son's education. Many of his engagement practices, although not often talked about as "parent involvement" at Grant Elementary, have been shown to matter for students of color in particular. They included vocalizing expectations of Gregorio going to college (Jeynes, 2010), providing real-world experiences of the harsh realities of working in manual labor to motivate Gregorio to focus on school (López, 2001), and developing his son's athletic and artistic abilities. The many sacrifices that Julio and Lucinda made as immigrants without documentation for their children's educational futures further illustrate the importance they gave to supporting their children's schooling and help debunk the myth that Latin@ immigrant parents do not care about their children's education.

Ideological Clarity: Ignacio

The case of Ignacio was somewhat different. Unlike most immigrant fathers at Grant, he asserted himself to open up spaces for his perspectives to be heard, and Ms. Vega viewed him as involved in his daughter's education. Yet the ways that he engaged in these relatively mainstream engagement practices were rejected by his daughter's teacher. Instead of being seen as supporting his daughter's education, he was seen as detracting from her academic development. It is useful to consider how Ignacio's family engagement practices—a serious demeanor, asking difficult questions to advocate for his daughter's academic development, and clear knowledge of his daughter's strengths and challenges—would have been understood and responded to if he were a White middle-class mother speaking in English rather than a Brown-skinned undocumented immigrant father from Mexico speaking in Spanish. His concerns about his daughter's learning were not taken seriously, and he was seen as overreacting and overbearing. It was not until Martina's 4th-grade year, after Ignacio and Alejandra had spent 5 years trying to advocate for increased attention to their daughter's learning, that educators suggested that Martina be tested for additional learning supports. By the end of 4th grade, Martina began to receive specialized services, and although her parents were frustrated that their concerns had been ignored for several years, they were relieved that educators were finally working with them to figure out Martina's learning challenges.

Developing Ideological Clarity

It is useful to consider what Ms. Vega could have done differently to begin to recognize fathers like Julio. One important step is overtly acknowledging the positions of power that most teachers hold vis-à-vis immigrant parents. Within face-to-face interactions, educators largely control the agenda, who gets to speak, and how contributions are evaluated. This entails great responsibility, because seemingly innocuous moves such as placing materials in front of mothers send messages that mothers are the only involved caregivers. Thus, small changes, such as intentionally making overt eye contact with all caregivers, can help open the conversation. To better recognize her own interactive patterns, Ms. Vega could videotape some of her own conferences and watch them to notice whom she speaks to, looks at, and responds to. Viewing her own conferences could help her notice that she rarely addressed fathers and that fathers rarely spoke. She could then implement intentional strategies, such as warmly asking fathers directly if they had thoughts regarding their child's schooling, and providing ample wait time for them to openly share their questions and perspectives.

For fathers like Ignacio, Ms. Vega could begin to develop ideological clarity by seeking out ways to disentangle caregivers' practices from her reactions to those practices. This is hard to do because these often exist below our level of consciousness and require purposeful examinations to reveal. Ethnographic researchers and educators who engage in funds of knowledge curriculum development take on approaches to achieve this (Moll et al., 1992). One strategy entails making a chart with two columns: one that lists the observable practices and a second that provides a space for evaluations and reactions to those observable practices. The two columns are necessary because, in everyday life, we tend to conflate what we notice and how we evaluate it, which leads us to understand what other people do based on our own upbringings of what we see is valuable and normal (Emerson, Fretz, & Shaw, 2011). By forcing ourselves to separate these two aspects, we can begin to recognize our own assumptions and evaluations. Although it would be impractical for educators to complete charts of this nature for every caregiver, it could be a useful approach to adopt with those caregivers with whom teachers sense tension. This is an activity that can be useful to try out with a trusted colleague as well. Often, outsiders can help understand our reactions and judgments in ways that we cannot disentangle ourselves. Developing ideological clarity requires reflection and often self-forgiveness, as it opens our eyes to the ways our everyday interactions reflect hierarchies in which we inadvertently participate.

Mexican immigrant fathers provide a powerful illustration of the need for humanizing family engagement because of the ways they are often overlooked or dehumanized in much of U.S. society today. Yet a humanizing approach does not matter only for Latino immigrant fathers. The African American families at Grant Elementary—who often differed from their children's teachers in terms of race, class, varieties of English, and formal education—were often positioned as uninvolved and as not caring about their children's education. As scholars such as Stuart Greene (2013) have shown, this is untrue, and critical approaches are needed to better understand the resources that families and minoritized children bring to their learning. Developing ideological clarity as a component of humanizing family engagement—in which we seek to question stereotypes and understand caregivers' practices from new perspectives—is the first component of an alternative, dynamic framework to begin explorations of how educators can learn from and with families in support of children's schooling.

PEDAGOGICAL TAKEAWAYS

- Make a list of caregivers from your classroom whom you view as involved and uninvolved.
  - ➢ What do you notice as you compare your two lists?
  - ➢ Are there some caregivers you have forgotten to include? Why do you think that is?
- Video record meetings or conferences that you have with your students' caregivers (with their permission). Take notes as you watch them.
  - ➢ What are things you do that you had not noticed during the interaction?
  - ➢ Who do you tend to speak to, share materials with, and make eye contact with?
  - ➢ What does your body language reveal?
  - ➢ Who asks questions? When do these questions become the focus of the dialogue?
- Seek out university students to help you transcribe the conferences and examine a transcript of the dialogue.
  - ➢ How often do you speak versus listen? How much talk time do caregivers have?

> ➤ What could you try differently during your next meetings to change these interactional patterns?
- Think of a caregiver you see as uninvolved or as detracting from his or her child's academic development.
  - ➤ Make a chart of the caregiver's observable practices separated from your reactions to his or her practices.
  - ➤ If possible, do this along with a trusted colleague and talk through your charts.
  - ➤ Reflect upon how this helps you understand the caregiver's practices from a different perspective.
- Collect all the handouts sent home to families over the course of a week. Look them over and consider the following:
  - ➤ What knowledges specific to U.S. schooling are required to make sense of each handout?
  - ➤ What abbreviations, proper nouns, technical language, or educational jargon are included?
  - ➤ If handouts are sent in multiple languages, what is the translation process, and how do you think it reflects the varieties of languages that your students' caregivers speak?
  - ➤ How can you tell when a handout is highly important or not?
  - ➤ What classroom systems could you develop to make handouts more accessible for immigrant families?

REFLECTION QUESTIONS

1. Think about a student's family member whom you view as being involved in schooling. Now think of one whom you view as not being involved.
   a. Discuss what has led you to these views, and on what approaches to parent involvement they may be based.
   b. Is there anything you wish you could know more about a student and his or her family in order to approach your collaboration with them differently?
2. Recognizing your own race, class, gender, and nation-based assumptions about good educational practices feels vulnerable and is difficult.
   a. How can you engage with educational materials and foster local educator inquiry groups to continually explore ways to develop your ideological clarity?
   b. How can you utilize these experiences to foster humanizing educational practices with students and families?

Chapter 3

Reimagining Home-Based Involvement

Fathers' Intentional Creation of
Alternative Learning Environments

Mateo (29 years old) and Susana (26 years old) were 2nd-grader Abi's parents, and were members of a mixed-status family in which Abi's U.S.-born brother Carlos (2 years old) was the only nuclear relative with U.S. documentation. Although it was a difficult decision to live apart for several years, like many with limited employment opportunities in Mexico, Mateo and Susana began working in Pennsylvania when Abi was a toddler. Abi remained in the care of her grandparents in Puebla until her mother returned to Mexico. When Abi was 4, she and her mother crossed the border to join Mateo in Marshall. He remembers being reunited with his young daughter and how it had initially felt strange because "she knew I was her dad, but she hadn't ever spent time with me." Abi also recalls their reunion, and her surprise when they told her that the guy with the long hair was her father. Their relationship quickly developed, Abi "*pegado*," or stuck to her father's side, as she got used to a new childhood in the United States.

Over the years, Susana had reliable work in food service, whereas Mateo's work varied seasonally, depending upon the availability of employment in landscaping and construction. Of the seven families from this study, two mothers and three fathers were the primary wage earners, and two couples were relatively equal in terms of their contributions to their family's income. Susana was a mother who contributed the majority to their family's income and, like almost half of the fathers, Mateo was the primary caretaker of his children after school and on the weekends. During many of my visits to their home, Susana was working, and it was common for Mateo to be cooking a meal, sweeping up the kitchen, and caring for his children. He reveled in teaching me—someone who was not yet a parent—how to change diapers and perform other caretaking practices. Susana worked long hours and sacrificed family time to make ends meet financially, which sometimes frustrated Mateo, who wished they could have more time together.

Like many immigrant families from this study, Mateo and Susana had initially planned to work in the United States for a few years before returning to

Mexico, and repatriation was a regular topic of conversation. Mateo had not seen his parents and siblings in nearly a decade, and longed to return to his life in Mexico. Abi, too, longed to see her grandparents and cousins, and to return to schools where she had felt successful at learning. During the spring of Abi's 1st-grade year, they made plans to return to Mexico the following December, after the summer and fall months when Mateo could save the most money. One afternoon, as Abi said good-bye to a classmate who was moving to a new school in Pennsylvania, she shared, "I'm going to Mexico, too. . . . I'm not going until December. When it starts to snow again, then I'll go. I'm leaving here." In the end, the family did not return to Mexico that December, although plans to potentially return were always in the works. Thus, as Mateo and Susana prepared for Abi's academic future, they thought about the skills and resources she would need to be successful in U.S. or Mexican schools.

By the time Abi was in 2nd grade, Mateo and his daughter had a close relationship—the two of them regularly engaged in playful arguments and teasing routines, and he boasted that his kids "were happiest by (his) side." He took tremendous pride in developing his children's Spanish skills, and Abi displayed the most extensive Spanish abilities of her classmates. Although his wife had more extensive English skills because of her work in customer service, Mateo's work and friendship networks primarily unfolded in Spanish. Because of her English abilities, Susana helped Abi with her homework on the evenings when she was home, although often Abi attempted assignments on her own. Mateo, who had a more flexible work schedule, attended most school events. Within their home, Mateo explicitly sought to create an environment that differed from school, where learning was based on real-world experiences.

This chapter shows how Mateo and his daughter's teacher, Mrs. Drescher, moved toward some aspects of humanizing family engagement. Through face-to-face interactions, he and Mrs. Drescher were able to establish relationships of mutual trust and were open to taking on the roles of expert and learner in which Abi's teacher expanded her understandings of who counted as involved. Yet there were other aspects of humanizing family engagement, such as an examination of what counts as involvement at home, that they did not broach. Mateo's engagement practices, or pedagogies of the home, illustrate how he sought to create a home learning environment that intentionally differed from the world of Abi's school. Through their experiences, this chapter invites readers to critically examine what counts as "good parent involvement." Rather than viewing families' un-school-like practices as signs of apathy toward their children's schooling, I show how these can be proactive choices that immigrant families tactically make in order to protect and educate their children. It is important for educators to critically question what counts as home-based engagement to move beyond the assumption that school-like homes are the only pathway for families and schools to support a child's education.

ABI ACROSS HOME AND SCHOOL CONTEXTS

Abi was an outgoing 2nd-grader who had had a bumpy transition into public schooling. Because of a positive screening for tuberculosis following her first days of kindergarten in Marshall, she had to miss the next several weeks until her treatment was complete. Because she had recently moved from Mexico, Grant's English-only model presented challenges for her. As a kindergartner, Abi was relatively disengaged with many of the classroom activities and often spoke of missing her grandparents in Mexico. She had low self-confidence about her English literacy skills and, throughout her early years in elementary school, talked openly about how she did not see herself as a good reader or writer. In an interview, she explained, "It's that I don't know how to read, but I'm trying." This contrasted with her incredible linguistic creativity and extensive oral abilities in Spanish—abilities that were widely unrecognizable to her English-speaking teachers at school. Outside of school, she loved telling stories and jokes, watching her favorite anime cartoons on YouTube, playing with her baby brother, and going on excursions with her father.

Abi became more engaged in schooling over the years, and by 2nd grade, she was an active participant in her classroom and ESL class, which she attended daily for 90 minutes. Approximately one-third of Grant Elementary students qualified for ESL services. These included pullout activities conducted in the hallway in kindergarten, carefully designed push-in writing classes that were cotaught between one classroom teacher per grade and the ESL teacher, and extensive 60- to 90-minute pullout literacy blocks taught by the ESL teacher in her classroom. Abi's 2nd-grade ESL teacher, Mrs. Cieza, worked with Abi and approximately 10 other 2nd-graders during this literacy block, nine of whom spoke Spanish as their home language. The class was conducted in English, although Mrs. Cieza knew Spanish as a second language. She would occasionally use Spanish as a support if children were unsure of the content in English, such as naming vocabulary in Spanish for clarification. Mrs. Cieza, an experienced, national board–certified ESL teacher, dedicated large amounts of time to coplan her pullout and push-in literacy curricula with classroom teachers and sought out regular scholarly and professional development opportunities.

Children in Abi's ESL class often drew upon their resources in Spanish and English to support their learning. For example, after a whole group read-aloud and discussion of Gary Soto's *Big Bushy Mustache* (1998) in English, Abi transitioned to a literacy center in which she played a version of bingo with digraphs (/th/, /sh/, and so on). As they played, Abi asked her tablemates, "Which one is 'wash'? *¿Cuál es esta palabra?*" (What's this word?), to which her classmate responded, "*No tienes*" (You don't have it). Unlike Mrs. Cieza, most classroom teachers did not have specific training to work with emergent bilingual students, and classes rarely incorporated language-based objectives tailored for bilingual students. In contrast, Mrs. Cieza's ESL literacy block followed the same literacy curriculum with adaptations to explicitly develop students' English language resources.

Abi's 2nd-grade classroom teacher was Mrs. Drescher. Mrs. Drescher was born and raised in Marshall and had been teaching at Grant Elementary for over 20 years. She showed her students tough love—her lessons would include moments of booming reprimands if students were off task as well as calling kids "honey" and joking with them. She also showed deep care for her students, seeking out resources and solutions to help them or their families in ways that surpassed many of her colleagues. The students who were considered disciplinary problems were often assigned to her, and most students were both terrified of her and adored her positive attention. She was not afraid to stray from the somewhat scripted curriculum, and would regularly break from the primary lesson goals to follow up on emergent themes or tell stories related to them. Unlike many of the younger and untenured teachers in the school, Mrs. Drescher was a veteran, tenured teacher who was in the new principal's good graces, and she did not appear concerned that she would be reprimanded for taking the time to develop cross-curricular or real-world connections.

In Mrs. Drescher's classroom of 22 students, Abi was one of 13 Latin@ immigrant students, 11 of whom had parents from Mexico and two from Puerto Rico. The remaining students were African American (7), White (1), or of African American and White heritage (1). Each student had an individual desk that held his or her belongings, which was occasionally susceptible to cleanliness checks by Mrs. Drescher. The desks formed an outside U, with interior rows, all of which faced the front whiteboard. The walls were adorned with exemplary student work and educational resources, a word wall, and a behavior management chart with each child's name on a clothespin that would be moved for misbehavior. In contrast to the earlier grades and Ms. Vega's classroom, the majority of the school day was spent in whole class, teacher-fronted lessons with some independent work at students' desks. Mrs. Drescher also welcomed additional adults in her classroom, and on a typical day it would be common to see resource teachers leading small-group instruction or Mrs. Drescher coteaching a literacy lesson with the ESL teacher. Although there were some learning centers, paired student work, and group science experiments, these were less typical than in other early-grade classrooms at Grant Elementary.

Mrs. Drescher did not know Spanish, but it was common for students to draw upon their resources in Spanish and English to support their learning in her room. For example, after Mrs. Drescher modeled a new math game called "What's Behind My Back," in which students worked in pairs with manipulatives to figure out basic subtraction, Abi was paired with another Mexican immigrant student. As they began Abi asked, "*¿Entonces cuántos me faltan?*" (So how many more do I need?) and counted aloud, "*Déjame contar, uno, dos, tres, cuatro, cinco*" (Let me count, one, two, three, four, five). When Mrs. Drescher arrived to work with this pair a few minutes later, Abi engaged in the same activity in English, thinking aloud as she solved the problem: "One, two, three, four, five, six. So, we need four more." Like most classroom teachers at Grant, Mrs. Drescher viewed many of her students from Latin@ families as "bilinguals in the making." She welcomed Spanish as an additional resource that her students could draw upon. Although students could draw upon the Spanish resources they already knew with classmates, in the English medium school there were no curricular opportunities for students to further develop their spoken Spanish or literacy. Therefore, students' development of resources in Spanish had to unfold in their homes and communities.

ESTABLISHING TRUSTING RELATIONSHIPS
DURING SCHOOL EVENTS

Mrs. Drescher met Abi's father, Mateo, through the traditional school event of parent–teacher conferences. Because of work schedules, Mateo attended the conference without his wife. Throughout the conference, he maintained a serious face, often focused on the details of the report card translated into Spanish. Later, he explained that he felt his serious face reflected the seriousness of the occasion—a one-on-one conference with his daughter's teachers. From his upbringing in Mexico, in which teachers usually met with parents as a collective, a personal meeting would have occurred only if the child did something wrong. Although his years as a parent at Grant Elementary had shaped his understanding of teacher conferences in the United States, he still felt that teachers should be treated with *respeto*, or deep respect. Mateo avoided direct eye contact with Mrs. Drescher, and despite his serious-looking demeanor, he also broke into regular smiles and occasional laughter that revealed hints of nervousness.

Throughout the conference, he agreed with what Mrs. Drescher and Mrs. Cieza said, and often added that he had noticed similar things about Abi at home. On one occasion, when the teachers highlighted that Abi was successful in math except with telling time on analog clocks, he politely interjected to share that "she already knows this . . . because now when I ask her 'What time is it?' now she can tell me." He illustrated that he monitored his daughter's academic growth and later brought up academic points he was hoping to focus on, such as helping with Abi's reading development. He explicitly asked if they had copies of leveled books that Abi could use to keep track of the words she had learned and which ones still confused her. Together, Mateo, Mrs. Drescher, and Mrs. Cieza came up with the idea of using corrective tape to mark these books.

In this meeting, Mrs. Drescher helped establish a space of *confianza* in which Mateo felt that he could risk naming the things that he was unsure of related to his daughter's schooling. She drew upon several important communicative strategies that helped her establish rapport with Mateo. Rapport is an important aspect of a humanizing approach because it provides a pathway for parents and teachers to get to know and trust one another as individuals. Mrs. Drescher spoke clearly, gestured, avoided educational jargon, and used the few Spanish words she knew. For example, in summarizing Abi's report card she shared, "One [as a grade] means we need to work on it. And you can see, no *unos* (ones)." Although it was a subtle difference, she also addressed Mateo directly as "you," rather than referring to him as "he" to the interpreter, something that rarely occurred with other teachers. She would look at Mateo and ask, "Do you have any questions?" rather than turning to the interpreter and saying, "Does he have any questions?" She set up her conference space so that she could make direct eye contact with her students' caregivers, and tried to make them all feel comfortable by sitting in "adult" chairs, rather than the miniature elementary school chairs. Unlike many other teachers, who subconsciously prioritized communication with mothers, Mrs. Drescher addressed all participants in her conferences, and the fact that Mateo attended conferences alone increased their opportunities to speak directly to one another. She also did something that many teachers rarely did: She welcomed Mateo to her classroom and thanked him for coming. Although this seems like something that would always occur, many teachers, often thrown off by the uncertainty of trying to determine if a parent would like to work with an interpreter, became flustered during the traditional greeting process and would dive directly into academic content without engaging in basic small talk. This was never malicious, but it serves as a useful reminder to be purposeful about relationship building.

Mrs. Drescher's conferences were reflective of her overall stated goals in which she emphasized the importance of establishing relationships of trust:

> I just try to be accepting. Let them know that it's okay if you can't say everything in English, that you can say it in Spanish and even like, write notes and we can find somebody to translate it. . . . I just try to be friendly, yet respectful. . . . I try to use that time to kind of get to know them. It's not much time to go over lots of specific things educationally. If I could form a bond where we can contact each other later and I give them a paper that says this and they see and they have questions, that they can feel comfortable to then ask me questions, I feel like I've done my job. I want them comfortable to come into the building. I want them coming back, I want them writing notes.

Her prioritizing of interpersonal relationships, developing trust, and seeking to learn across difference contrasts dramatically with the behavior of most other teachers at Grant Elementary. Although many other teachers wanted to foster collaborations with parents, the form and content of their interactions with parents inadvertently positioned the teacher as expert and the parent as learner. Mrs. Drescher's conferences, in contrast, tended to rely less on formal documents to guide the conferences, and she spent a large portion of the time trying to talk with parents in order to get to know them on a personal level. Overall, her conferences were less scripted than those of most other teachers, who tended to discuss the same topics in the same sequence with similar wording.

By the end of Mrs. Drescher's first conference with Mateo, she highlighted that Abi's growth so far that year was "wonderful" and emphasized to Mateo, "You're doing a great job." Mateo smiled warmly and thanked her for her hard work in Abi's learning. Mrs. Drescher's approach to parent–teacher conferences facilitated the development of interpersonal relationships of trust, a key facet of humanizing family engagement.

Mrs. Drescher's establishment of a trusting relationship with Mateo also provided opportunities for her to begin to develop as a learner. This happened in terms of whom she started to view as an engaged parent. Historically, the population at Grant Elementary, which was zoned for low-income rentals in the city center, had been almost entirely African American, and in an interview, Mrs. Drescher shared that many African American students earlier in her career did not have fathers who attended school events. The rapid growth in the Latin@ immigrant population at Grant, which housed the largest Latin@ population in the district, had occurred since 2005. It was common for fathers from Latin@ families to attend school events because of engagement in their children's schooling, daytime work schedules in which they were more likely than their spouse to have evenings free, differences in English resources compared with their spouses, and other factors. In the months prior to this conference in 2008, Mrs. Drescher tended to only name mothers as the recipients and responsible parties for home–school relationships. After conferences, however, she noted how she was surprised that Mateo had come alone and she began to reference both Abi's mom and dad when talking about family engagement. During informal interviews with me, Mrs. Drescher also reflected on my presence in her classroom. She saw me as a resource to get to know and ask general questions about Spanish-speaking families, which provided a space for her to notice, learn, and reflect upon her students' caregivers in new ways.

Through her development of a trusting relationship with Mateo, Mrs. Drescher also became a learner in terms of the ways that a family's documentation status could shape school-based practices. One day, she was going through students' take-home folders and Abi's had not been checked by anyone at home. She did not know the documentation status of Abi's family, and as a public school teacher, she knew she could not ask them, but she had learned in recent conversations that Abi's parents were having a difficult time getting Abi's bus changed for their new address. As undocumented immigrants, they had not yet been able to get bills in their own names to prove that they belonged to their new catchment area. This meant Mateo was walking Abi to and from school on the days they could not have a friend give her a ride. Instead of reprimanding Abi for not doing her "job" of making sure her family looked at the papers in her folder, as she often did when folders went untouched, Mrs. Drescher explained that she knew Abi must have been in a rush that morning and she understood that her father may not have had time. This typical school-based interaction further highlights ways that Mrs. Drescher began to incorporate fathers' engagement in their children's schooling, by naming Abi's father in home–school engagement practices.

The humanizing relationship that Mrs. Drescher began to establish with Mateo continued throughout the school year, such as during other conferences that he attended without his wife. Mateo and Mrs. Drescher's communication unfolded in similar ways: He maintained a serious face with limited eye contact, he largely agreed with what Mrs. Drescher said and offered similar observations that he had noticed at home, and his serious demeanor gave way to warm smiles.

The following excerpt from their spring conference illustrates the ways that Mrs. Drescher (Mrs. D) and Mateo moved toward humanizing family engagement within this interaction. Mrs. Drescher gave Mateo a routine letter from the nurse about Abi's body mass index and explained that it was nothing to be worried about. They both agreed that Abi was bigger than most children, but she would grow into her body. Mateo then commented about Abi's participation in sports with him:

> *Mateo: De todos modos los domingos hace deportes conmigo.* (Anyway, on Sundays she plays sports with me.)
> ((Translation))
> *Mrs. D:* Good. Aww, soccer?
> *Mateo:* Uh-huh.
> *Mrs. D:* Aah. Where do you play?
> ((Translation))
> *Mateo: Aquí en, ¿cómo se llama? Cuatrocincuentados en Siracusa.* (Here in, what's it called? 452 in Siracusa.)
> *Mrs. D:* Oh, Siracusa. 452 Sports Complex.
> *Mateo:* Yeah.
> *Mrs. D:* My son played lacrosse there. (Gestures cradling lacrosse ball.)
> *Mateo:* Yeah? (Smiling at Mrs. D.)

In this interaction, despite limited shared linguistic resources in English and Spanish, Mateo and Mrs. Drescher were able to establish direct communication about a sports complex. More important, they were able to get to know each other as well as find things they had in common. Mrs. Drescher was also able to learn about some of the activities in which Mateo engaged Abi. This type of direct personal communication rarely unfolded between Mexican immigrant fathers and teachers, and illuminates the subtle ways that Mrs. Drescher and Mateo moved toward humanizing engagement.

Viewing Mateo as deeply engaged in his daughter's schooling may have also impacted Mrs. Drescher's beliefs about Abi's academic future. In an interview about the study's students, she named Abi as one of the two she imagined continuing on to college. When asked why, she explained that it was because she viewed Abi's family (even naming Mateo) as "caring more about furthering an education past high school" and "because they just push her so." Based on school assessments, Abi was among the least academically successful students in the grade, yet because of her parents' (and predominantly her father's) support, Mrs. Drescher imagined her continuing on to college. Mrs. Drescher had not spoken with Abi's mom, so this impression was largely based on her meetings with Mateo.

Through their in-person interactions Mrs. Drescher and Mateo illustrated how to engage in two aspects of humanizing family engagement: fostering relationships of trust to get to know each other as individuals and each taking on the role of a learner. Through these actions, Mrs. Drescher began to expand who counted as involved in a child's schooling, moving from a heavy emphasis on mothers to the inclusion of fathers. She also began to learn about some of the realities immigrant families faced related to schooling.

In terms of school-based engagement, she noticed Mateo and viewed him as involved. Yet her view of home-based engagement practices was relatively traditional—in which parents helped with homework, supported their children's literacy development by reading with them and monitoring their reading logs, and supporting their academic abilities in English. Mateo's home-based engagement practices, in which he strategically sought out ways to create an alternative home-based learning environment that differed from Abi's English medium schooling, instead prioritized developing Spanish language resources and experiential learning. He did not engage in these educational practices because he was ignorant about desired parent involvement practices in the United States. Instead, he made these intentional moves to ensure that his daughter would foster a positive sense of self as a Mexican immigrant child and develop resources for a successful academic future in either the United States or Mexico.

MATEO'S ENGAGEMENT ACROSS CONTEXTS: HOMES ARE NOT SCHOOLS

Mrs. Drescher presumed that a father she viewed as highly engaged in school-based events also took on what she considered highly engaged practices at home. In this section, I shift the focus to Abi's home to show the strategic tactics Mateo drew upon to intentionally foster a home learning environment that differed from English medium schooling, and how he pushed against the notion that children's homes should be an extension of their school-based learning.

Unlike the overlapping spheres model of parent involvement described by Epstein (2010), in which the de facto presumption is that homes should become like mainstream schools and parents should take on teacher-like practices, Mateo's orientation to family engagement included maintaining a home environment that was distinct from Abi's schooling context. His practices were more reflective of Doucet's (2011b) work with Haitian immigrant families, in which families constructed intentional boundaries between their children's home and school worlds to enhance their education and well-being. Like Mateo, the participants from Doucet's study were not indifferent about their children's education, as they were often assumed to be. Through a window into Mateo and Abi's home-based practices, I illustrate how Mateo intentionally avoided learning spaces in which school-based activities such as homework shaped how they spent their time, the roles they took on, and the status that parents and children were assigned based on their abilities to help with assignments in English.

Family Language Policy

One way that Mateo was engaged in his daughter's education was through intentional home-based language policies that complimented her English medium schooling to develop her bilingualism. Language policies are the explicit and implicit rules and practices regarding acceptable languages within given contexts. Although Grant Elementary never established an official English-only policy, the de facto language of schooling was English. All instruction, materials, and assessments were conducted in English, overlooking the bilingual resources that almost half of all students brought to their classrooms. Abi's home, in contrast, had a family language policy that sought to protect the value and development of Spanish. According to Fogle (2013), "family language policy refers to explicit and overt decisions parents make about language use and language learning as implicit processes that legitimize certain language and literacy practices over others in the home" (p. 83). Mateo was attuned to local and national language ideologies, or beliefs about languages and their speakers, that elevated the importance of English and often belittled the value of Spanish and its speakers (Arzubiaga & Adair, 2010; Gallo et al., 2014). He also knew many children from Mexican immigrant families who could no longer communicate with their relatives in Spanish. Because he saw that Abi was learning English at school and in the larger community, he adopted a family language policy that prioritized Spanish in order to expose his children to both languages and develop their bilingualism. As many scholars in bilingualism have shown, Mateo believed that a strong foundation in the first language would increase children's language and literacy development in both English and Spanish (e.g., Thomas & Collier, 1997).

The following interaction illustrates the ways in which beliefs about the value of English and Spanish permeated Mateo and Abi's lives, and the way that English was often viewed as more important in Marshall. Generally, Mateo spoke only Spanish with his children, expected them to speak Spanish with him, and regularly engaged in Spanish medium media on the television and computer. Thus, Abi usually spoke Spanish at home and delighted in developing her Spanish resources with her father. Out of all the students in this study, she spoke most candidly about her fears of forgetting Spanish. In an interview, she shared, "If I forget my Spanish, I won't be able to speak with my family, and my family is most important to me." Yet Abi also understood the value of knowing English in the United States, and one afternoon she was upset with her father for not taking her on an outing to a store. In protest, she intentionally started shouting at him in English, the language of power and authority in their Pennsylvania town, to which he gently responded, *"Habla español, hija"* (Speak Spanish, honey). He continued by reasoning "You have to speak Spanish because there are parents who don't speak English at all, my love. They are not going to understand what you say." Abi, looking to wield the power of English over her father, responded, "Hello, Dad! My mom speak English and you don't speak!" In a calm voice, Mateo continued to reason with Abi, who had had uncomfortable experiences in her first years in Marshall when kids made fun of her for not knowing English well. He asked if she would like people to speak to her in a language she didn't understand. In protest, Abi continued in English, rolling her eyes as she told him, "I will not care." Through these conversations, Mateo sought to provide moral lessons on not using language as a tool of discrimination.

Yet he was also pushing against a sociolinguistic context in which knowing English was seen as highly desirable. At times, Abi mentioned that her father was *"burro"* (dumb) because he didn't know English, illustrating her exposure to, and partial belief that, speaking English was associated with intelligence whereas Spanish referenced ignorance (Zentella, 2003). Mateo had developed moderate abilities in English, yet he also feigned absolute incomprehension of English with his children to create a context in which they had to speak Spanish to communicate with him. Like other bilingual families seeking to restrict their children's loss of their home language (Shin, 2013), Mateo adopted creative family language policies to foster an environment in which his children would experience authentic reasons to develop their Spanish. Thus, part of his engagement practices entailed strategically resisting English as the language of their home, and developing Abi's tools to see bilingualism, and knowing Spanish, as normal and desirable. His family language policies were not because he could not speak English. Instead, they were calculated tactics to develop his daughter's bilingualism, educational resources that he saw as necessary for her successful future in the United States, or Mexico, if the family decided to return.

Mrs. Drescher was not opposed to children speaking Spanish at home or school, yet she did not understand the tremendous educational work required of caregivers to develop children's Spanish in an environment that celebrated English monolingualism. In addition, her classroom-based response to complicated bilingual situations was to avoid discomfort and prioritize English monolingualism. For example, she encouraged students to speak English if a monolingual English speaker was present so that they would not feel left out, but did not engage students in dialogue about linguistic difference. She also shared how she worried about students from monolingual English-speaking homes trying to speak Spanish, as she thought that it might come across in a "mocking sense" (see Link, Gallo, & Wortham, 2014). Her response, in an understandable move to make sure no one was being disrespected, was to tell non-Latin@ students that if they did not know Spanish, they should not speak it. This contrasts with Mateo's approach, in which he engaged his daughter in conversations about linguistic difference and discrimination. Although not often considered a form of family school engagement, Mateo's strategic language policies were crucial resources that supported Abi's education.

Intentional Constructions of Nonschool Learning

Another way that Mateo was engaged in Abi's education was through strategically resisting school-like learning routines within their home. Typical home-based family engagement practices often assume that parents are responsible for creating school-like learning environments in which activities such as English medium homework shape how families spend their time and the status they are assigned based on their abilities to help with homework (Mangual Figueroa, 2011). Mateo preferred to maintain a home that was based on experiential learning rather than routine academic procedures of English phonemic awareness flashcards or writing number stories. Abi's parents had a vision of education in which they regularly attributed Abi's academic growth to the fact that her father found ways to remove the stress of traditional academics and schooling, and instead engaged in real-world learning. Like many humanizing pedagogy scholars, Mateo was critical of the purely academic focus at Abi's school and did not want to turn their home into an extension of the school day, where knowledge and worth were measured by standards, testing, or expertise in academic English.

Mateo used several similar interactional moves to avoid school-based activities at home. These included direct statements like "It's Sunday; leave school at school," strategic humor to change the subject, and feigned lack of comprehension in English or mock boredom when Abi discussed school-based topics. One weekend morning, Abi searched for her schoolbooks and reading log, where she was supposed to record all of her reading. If she completed the log, she could attend a party at school. Like most children who had only experienced "reading logs" in English, she was unsure what to call this activity in Spanish, and she continually told her father, "*Estoy buscando mi* reading log" (I'm looking for my reading log). In a playful back-and-forth, he exhibited a dramatic yawn as she kept explaining her reading log in English, and she dramatically swatted his leg in annoyance. He acted as if he had no idea what she was talking about because she could not explain it in Spanish, although he illustrated his understanding of this activity several weeks later during conferences, when he asked Abi's teachers about the reading log, or what he described as "the sheet of paper where she [Abi] writes down the names of books that I have to sign." This interaction illustrates that he was not oblivious to traditional school-based engagement practices, but instead purposefully sought out ways to avoid them to prioritize other forms of learning.

Humanizing family engagement, which demands that educators critically examine what counts as involvement, helps us understand the ways in which Mateo did see himself as being engaged in Abi's schooling in innovative ways. He explained, "With homework, well, I pretty much don't have time. Her mom does more of that." Yet there were ways he was engaged in her school-based academic learning, especially when they related to authentic, real-world topics. For instance, he brought up how, during the conference several days beforehand, Abi's teachers thought she did not know how to read an analog clock. He explained:

> With her mom, she got confused. With me, Abi asked me how the clock worked because it has those numbers. I tried to explain to her that every number has a space of five, etc. I kept explaining it to her and then I said, "What time is it?" and she said, "Quarter past two" or "two fifteen." And now she actually says to me, "Hey, is it X o'clock?" Explaining things to her takes more time. In things like this, that her mom can't understand, she addresses them with me. But I try to make it fun, taking our time, with patience.

Mateo prioritized authentic learning, and his engagement practices prioritized enjoying the process of learning, rather than the task of completing homework. Occasionally, this overlapped with the learning goals of Abi's schooling and homework. Unfortunately, most of Abi's school-based assignments focused on repetitive, isolated practice of letters, sounds, and math skills. Mateo actively decided not to engage in this form of family school engagement.

Mateo also mentioned how advice giving was a core component of his engagement in Abi's education. He explained, "I give her *consejos* (advice). I explain to her what things are right. . . . In things that her mom can't see, she gets guidance from me." As Guadalupe Valdés (1996) illustrated in her foundational work with Mexican immigrant mothers, *consejos* were a fundamental way that caregivers from Mexico educate their children. Mateo and other fathers illustrate that in many Mexican immigrant families today, it is not just mothers who are positioned as responsible for children's education and advice giving, but also fathers. In his explanation of *consejos*, Mateo talked about the importance of relationships of *confianza* with his daughter—something that he saw as a foundation to guide her choices and foster a relationship with her in which she could be open with him.

Mateo's engagement practices undergirded her school-based learning, as Abi regularly embedded things she learned from his real-world teaching into her classroom practices. Her father loved to talk to her about scientific concepts, such as the solar system or animals. One day, Abi sat with three Latin@ classmates and they selected a nonfiction book from the class library about reptiles.

When they got to the page about snakes, kids started sharing things they knew, and Abi commanded the floor to explain how snakes are able to smell. Abi explained that she knew this because, "My dad told me that they stick out their tongue so they can taste and smell outside." In a school where the science curriculum was largely eradicated in the early grades to prioritize the assessed subjects of literacy and math, Abi's scientific learning was largely being developed with her father.

Abi regularly drew upon her experiences with her father as the basis for her writing as well. Several of her stories related to family trips to the river, where her father taught them how to swim. One afternoon, Abi began writing about a time when she lost her flip-flop, first drawing a picture with a huge wave and then carefully sounding out the letters to write, "I lost my shoe in the water." When I asked her about her story so that she could add more details, she explained with enthusiasm:

> And then I run because I was—the water get more bigger. And this water was going to get down to my face, that's why I was running. . . . (Switching to Spanish.) But then he [my dad] almost grabbed my flip-flop because it was floating away from me. . . . Then I saw it high up on the wave, and I said, "That's why I can't get it." . . . I went after it. My flip-flop was floating. And then when the wave came, it carried it down the river.

When I asked her father about this story in an interview, he reminisced about the infamous flip-flop. Like Abi, he incorporated suspenseful details and direct quotes as he recounted:

> The sparkly sandal went from above to below, but the current was strong. There went her sandals, and she [Abi] shouted, "Aaaa, my flip flop!" And there I go, chasing the flip-flop. But this water was strong and it broke her flip-flop. Yes, it's rare—it broke her flip-flop! Her flip-flop was broken, and we ended up having to throw it out. That was back when we used to go swimming, when we had a car.

Mateo was a masterful storyteller and, as is reflected in their similar narrative styles, he often modeled and developed these language and literacy skills with Abi. Logistical details, such as being able to afford a car to get places like a nearby river to swim, also shaped the opportunities that immigrant parents had to engage in what they saw as educational activities. Mateo did not take his children to science centers or museums, a family-based educational practice that is often lauded as supportive of children's education (Fenichel & Schweingruber, 2010). The exorbitant costs of transportation and entrance fees for such places in the nearby city were not attainable for most families. In addition, most children's museums are geared toward English-speaking, middle-class families, and many immigrant families feel alienated in such spaces (Fenichel & Schweingruber, 2010).

Mateo's pedagogies of the home, instead, centered on authentic learning experiences, developing Abi's Spanish resources, and guiding her choices through advice giving. Unlike traditional home-based involvement practices, such as homework centered on practicing isolated English literacy skills in which parents were supposed to take on teacher-like roles, Mateo intentionally engaged in an array of educational practices that were notably absent from her schooling. Mrs. Drescher would not have been opposed to Mateo's engagement practices. In fact, as someone who regularly sought out ways to make personal and world-based connections to classroom content, she would have been interested in learning about and building upon Mateo's engagement practices. Yet she did not have opportunities to do this.

TOWARD HUMANIZING FAMILY ENGAGEMENT: WHAT COUNTS AS PARENT INVOLVEMENT

During their limited face-to-face interactions at school events, Mrs. Drescher and Mateo successfully moved toward humanizing family engagement in large part because of Mrs. Drescher's intentional strategies that prioritized getting to know parents as individuals. Rather than cramming a litany of standards, assessments, and educational jargon into a 15-minute meeting, she provided a brief overview of each student's school-based learning and then sought out ways to talk with caregivers. She established this through the content of her talk—asking genuine questions about their lives and reciprocally sharing her own life— as well as through interactional strategies such as addressing family members directly. She established the foundations of a trusting relationship and opened herself up as a learner rather than only as an expert, and through this process she started to notice new things about her students' educational lives. By getting to know Mateo, she began to better recognize a father's engagement practices as well as the ways that students' experiences as immigrants shape their schooling.

Mateo's home-based engagement practices show that supporting a child's schooling may entail a range of activities that differ from things that are often considered "good parent involvement." Mateo's decisions to avoid English medium homework and reading were not because he lacked an understanding of U.S.-based involvement practices. Instead, he believed that they were not the best way he could support his daughter's education, and he actively sought out ways to engage in alternative educational activities. These included family language policies where developing Spanish was valued and necessary, authentic learning opportunities that Abi applied during her school-based practices, and advice giving so that she could navigate her surroundings as a Mexican immigrant student from an undocumented family. Fathers like Mateo illustrate that school-like homes are not the only pathway for families and schools to support a child's education.

Rather than starting from a laundry list of traditional family engagement practices to check off what nonmainstream parents are doing, we should instead start from an understanding of how parents see themselves as engaged in their children's education. As illustrated by the diverse ways in which Mateo, Julio, and Ignacio supported their children's schooling, this happens in ways that cannot be simplified into essentializing "best practices," in which all Mexican fathers engage in a list of practices. Prioritizing a limited view of involvement is not the best way to support children who bring a wide range of educational resources from their homes. Rather than ignoring these ranges of resources, I suggest that teachers seek out ways to understand and use them to determine alternative pathways to meet learning goals in their classrooms.

Accessing Alternative Home-Based Engagement Practices

It is useful to consider what teachers like Mrs. Drescher could do to better access the home-based engagement practices of diverse caregivers. An important point of departure is explicitly naming what she sees as desirable home-based engagement practices, and why. She could achieve this by creating a chart with three columns: one where she lists each of her desired engagement practices, a second where she explains why she believes they support students' schooling, and a third where she explores other possibilities that might help her reach similar learning goals. When teachers are given the space to interrogate the list of practices that they assume are important, they can begin to imagine new possibilities and consider a wider range of engagement practices.

Mrs. Drescher could also seek out ways to learn from diverse caregivers and engage in open conversations with them about how they see themselves as supporting their children's education. This is likely something Mrs. Drescher would do well, based on her ability to engage in authentic conversations in which she puts caregivers at ease and seeks to learn about their lives. As she did when she learned about the ways Mateo plays sports with Abi, she could ask caregivers questions such as "What types of things do you like to do with [child] when you're together?" or "What are things that you like to do that you think help support his or her schooling?" As the 1st-grade teachers from Chapter 1 illustrated, inviting parents into the classroom to share their interests and visiting them in their homes to learn from them are additional ways that Mrs. Drescher could begin to learn more about families' engagement practices.

Another possibility includes building upon the Mexican schooling tradition of forming a caregiver committee that helps shape classroom decisions. As my current study in Mexican primary schools illustrates, a *comité de padres de familia*, (parent committee) is commonplace in most Mexican schools, and this group fosters relationships with classroom teachers and administrators in order to support and inform schooling decisions. This committee can provide feedback on homework practices, help plan family events, suggest excursions reflective of the authentic learning practices engaged in by families, and serve as a sounding board for enhancing family–school relationships. As educators, we have things to learn from immigrant parents, as well as the schooling systems they have grown up in, and many Mexican schools provide a useful example of how teachers and parents come together to support children's learning both inside and outside the classroom.

PEDAGOGICAL TAKEAWAYS

- Collect and look through the homework you have sent home in the past week.
  - ➤ What types of learning does it prioritize? Is it mostly isolated practice of school-based skills, or are there opportunities to engage in authentic learning practices?
  - ➤ In what languages is homework written? How do you think those who read other languages make sense of the assignments?
  - ➤ What role do you want caregivers to play in homework completion, and why?
  - ➤ How do you provide feedback on completed homework? How do caregivers or students clearly know that they have completed it adequately?
- Be purposeful in your face-to-face communication with immigrant parents.
  - ➤ Address them directly as "you," not as "him" or "her" through an interpreter.
  - ➤ Orient your eye gaze and body language to family members—think about all the ways we build rapport in conversation that are not about the content of our words.
  - ➤ Minimize your use of technical jargon, handouts, reports, and charts.
  - ➤ If you know some words in a language they speak, try to integrate those words. Most caregivers appreciate the effort and your lack of expertise in their language helps balance power differentials.
- Visit a local museum geared toward children and think about the following:
  - ➤ How do you get there via public transportation?
  - ➤ How much does it cost for a family of five to visit? Are there special discounts available to supplement this cost?
  - ➤ What do you notice about the demographics of families visiting this space?
  - ➤ What languages are the signs and educational information written in? How do you think families that read languages other than English would experience this space?

REFLECTION QUESTIONS

1. How do you design and implement face-to-face interactions such as conferences to get to know caregivers as people?
   a. What goals do you have?
   b. How can you design these interactions better to meet humanizing goals?
2. What do you assume are important home-based engagement practices?
   a. Why do you believe they are important?
   b. What are ways that you have learned from your students' families to enhance the students' school-based learning?
   c. If you are having a difficult time thinking of examples, what are ways that you could create opportunities to listen and learn from them and incorporate this into your pedagogy?

Chapter 4

Superdaddy's *Buena Educación* and Lessons on Linguistic Appropriateness

Emily was a 2nd-grader in Mrs. Drescher's class whose parents, Cristián and Paloma, grew up with limited financial resources in a small town in Puebla, Mexico. Similar to many Mexicans from rural towns of their generation, they had attended school through the 6th grade and then had to leave because their families could not afford to pay the costs associated with their schooling. Cristián (30 years old), a clean-cut and charismatic man with dark wavy hair and a contagious smile, moved to Marshall for work opportunities in his late teenage years. During a brief return to his hometown, he and Paloma (27 years old) began dating and they returned to Marshall together. Paloma had a daughter from a previous relationship, whom she left in her mother's care until she could bring her to Pennsylvania. In Marshall, their daughter Emily (8 years old) was born, and several years later their son Cristofer (1 year old) added to their family. Emily was in regular contact with her sister and grandma in Mexico, and she met them for the first time the summer after her 2nd-grade year.

As with many families, their home and work responsibilities did not represent static or traditional gender roles, such as stay-at-home moms and breadwinner fathers. Instead, they continually changed based on employment opportunities and family needs. For many years both parents worked several jobs and shared child-care duties. Once Emily's baby brother was born, they decided that Cristián would work two full-time jobs, as his advanced spoken English abilities meant he could earn more as a manager for office cleaning services at night and as a landscaper during the day. Even with his exhausting work schedule, Cristián prioritized time with his family. He explained:

> I have always tried to do good things with my children. For example, I am strict with them, I am patient with them. . . . Emily, I hug her every day. I spoil her every day. I tell her that she is very important for me. That's it. She is a part of me. She is like my hand. If she is sick, it hurts me. If she is sad, I am sad. . . . I want her to feel protected by me. I want to be her Superman. I want to be her Superman always. Her Superdaddy.

Unlike his own father, who had not been affectionate or spent much time with him growing up, Cristián tried to schedule one morning off a week so he could cook a lavish breakfast for his family, walk Emily to the bus stop, or take both children camping on the weekend. He loved the outdoors, cultivating their small garden, and watching cooking shows so he could experiment with new recipes. He also saw it as his responsibility to make sure his children were *bien educado*, or well educated and moral (Arzubiaga & Adair, 2010; Valdés, 1996), which for him entailed making conscious choices for appropriate behavior and language.

In this chapter, I show how Cristián's school engagement reflected notions of *una buena educación* (a good education), which included explicit lessons and implicit modeling of how to be a linguistically appropriate bilingual speaker. His lessons about metalinguistic awareness[1]—or knowledge about how languages work and interrelate— provided crucial strategies for his daughter that helped her leverage her bilingual resources for language and literacy learning. As leading scholars in bilingual education have shown, metalinguistic awareness should be a component of school-based literacy curricula because teaching children to notice similarities and differences across their language systems (for example, English and Spanish) has important academic benefits, such as improved phonological awareness and the ability to transfer conceptual knowledge and skills across languages (Escamilla et al., 2014). Metalinguistic awareness, like many literacy strategies, is not innate, and is more effectively used when taught. Although more than half of Emily's classmates came from bilingual homes, their school-based literacy curriculum did not explicitly foster students' development of metalinguistic awareness. Emily's development in this area relied on her father's home-based language and literacy pedagogies. As part of humanizing family engagement, teachers can learn from families' language and literacy approaches—such as developing students' metalinguistic awareness—and should seek out ways to incorporate these pedagogies into their school-based literacy instruction to support children's bilingual and biliterate potential.

EMILY'S LITERACY LEARNING ACROSS HOME AND SCHOOL CONTEXTS

Emily was a cheerful 8-year-old with a strong moral compass who was regularly seen as a model student within school. Unlike many other students from Mexican immigrant families, Emily excelled in English medium literacy at school and was an enthusiastic reader. She did not, however, know how to read or write in Spanish, and she imagined her sister in Mexico would one day teach her. She was a tall and sturdy girl, often dressed in sporty pink outfits, and she stood up for others when she saw something unjust. She was well liked by students and teachers and excelled academically. At home, she loved to help out with her little brother or talk to her sister in Mexico on the phone. She had her own bedroom filled with toys, such as a pink karaoke machine and a plastic kitchenette where she and her father had tea parties with the clay cups that her grandmother had sent from Mexico. She loved to sing, play doctor, and stay up late reading library books under the covers with a flashlight.

Questioning What Counts as Literacy

The literacy curriculum that Emily experienced during her first 3 years at Grant Elementary was taught only in English, changed annually, and by her 2nd-grade year, was largely reflective of the conventional literacy skills endorsed by the National Reading Panel (2000), the report used to inform federal literacy initiatives under No Child Left Behind. These included skills such as phonemic awareness (identifying and manipulating phonemes, or the smallest sound units that can differentiate meaning), phonics (understanding the relationships between sounds and spelling patterns), fluency (reading quickly, accurately, and with expression), and comprehension (processing a text and understanding its meaning). Rather than prioritizing authentic literacy practices that had real-world purposes or audiences (Genishi & Dyson, 2009), the curriculum increasingly focused on discrete skills that were usually taught and assessed in isolation from one another. As a Title I school that worked with predominantly low-income Latin@ immigrant and African American students, Grant Elementary faced increasing pressures to meet benchmark goals on standardized assessments. These assessments often measured students' performance of the discrete skills that came to dominate the curriculum, such as decoding, oral reading fluency, and phonemic awareness. In 2009, the new superintendent from a large, urban district pressured principals to replace more balanced approaches—which taught literacy through a combination of authentic practices and discrete skills—with skills-based, packaged curricula. In 2010, the superintendent replaced the long-standing principal at Grant with someone from the superintendent's previous district, and additional curricular changes ensued. Teachers spent extensive time learning the new packaged curricula, and lamented that by the time they had a grasp of the new materials, the curriculum would change again. Over the 3 years that I spent observing classrooms at Grant Elementary, the literacy curriculum increasingly restricted what counted as literacy, and the dominant approaches did not take into account the home-based literacy practices of many students.

What counts as literacy, and how it is taught in schools, is shaped by ideologies. There is no singular "best" way to develop literacy, and this chapter invites readers to consider a range of literacy practices that are less frequently recognized and built upon in schools, yet are nonetheless practices that have served generations of families from diverse backgrounds. I challenge readers to critically examine the literacy measures used in their local educational contexts and to consider how a broader range of literacy practices could be tapped to meet school-based literacy goals. To best support minoritized students' literacy development, we must learn from their home-based literacy practices and then use that knowledge to help students expand their literacy repertoires (Genishi & Dyson, 2009; Heath, 1983; Orellana & D'warte, 2010). This is not to suggest that conventional literacy skills are unimportant, as developing abilities such as sound-letter correspondence is useful for students' English literacy learning. What it does say, however, is that these conventional skills cannot be the only literacy practices that count, and that a more effective approach to literacy development would recognize and build upon the range of literacy practices and strategies that minoritized students bring to school (Orellana & D'warte, 2010). This chapter focuses on the experiences of Emily and her father to envision how practices in support of one important literacy resource—developing metalinguistic awareness—could be incorporated into school-based literacy instruction. At the end of the chapter, I suggest other diverse pedagogies that can support students' literacy development.

Increasingly Restrictive Literacy Curricula at Grant Elementary

During Emily's kindergarten year, before administrative changes at the district level, the literacy curriculum integrated more holistic approaches to literacy (writing based on kids' experiences, authentic children's literature through whole class read-alouds) with discrete emergent literacy skills. These included rhymes, beginning sounds, blending sounds, and segmenting sounds. Students were regularly assessed on these emergent literacy skills, and the focus of kindergarten conferences entailed reports of how many skills a student had mastered.

Even before the district began to make changes, homework largely focused on daily book reading and practicing isolated skills through flashcards and worksheets in English. Although teachers assumed these were basic literacy skills that all parents could easily help with, parents who were Spanish dominant experienced extensive stress and difficulty engaging with these emergent literacy homework activities in English. For example, the flashcard for the letter *I* had a picture of a monkey scratching its fur, from which the parent or child was supposed to deduce the /i/ for *itch*. On worksheets, there were pictures of slacks and slippers, without the written words, and students had to determine the appropriate consonant blends to add (for example, /bl/ or /sl/). These were challenging for Spanish-dominant caregivers for several reasons: They often included relatively obscure vocabulary, such as *slacks*, rather than the more common word *pants* that would be familiar to immigrant families. The practice activities also focused on the form of words, the goal of the activity. Yet, because the words were presented in isolation from any meaningful context, readers were not able to draw upon context cues to figure out the meaning or anticipated form. Finally, because English has a complex pronunciation system (for instance, *father*, *able*, and *pirate* all have different /a/ sounds) compared with Spanish (which has close to a one-to-one correspondence of letters and sounds), parents were uncertain of how to discern the precise phonemic sounds that the practice drills demanded. Although many families were unsure about these activities, they rarely voiced their concerns because they worried it would cause them to look unintelligent or unsupportive of their children's schooling.

Emily's parents were unsure of how to help with these assignments, and requested time off from work to be able to participate in a pilot initiative in which Spanish-speaking families, teachers, and university researchers came together once a week to support families' questions related to homework and schooling (see Gallo, Wortham, & Bennett, 2015). Other Spanish-dominant families did not fare as well. Some worried they would cause their children more harm than good by trying to help with this narrow version of skills-based practice in English. Others endured teasing from their children when they were unable to reproduce the highly specific phonemic sounds that their children had learned for each letter. Just as teachers often did not recognize the specificity of the isolated literacy skills, repetitive school-based practice normalized this version of literacy as simple and common sense for many children. Those who could not perform these sound patterns well—such as their parents, or certain students—were thus positioned as unintelligent.

In 1st grade, students learned through a writer's workshop curriculum, based on authentic writing practices, and conferenced with their teachers regarding their stories and poetry. Students still practiced emergent literacy skills that isolated surface-level skills from meaningful contexts, and each week they were given different sight words to memorize. By 2nd grade, with the arrival of the new principal, the school adopted a semi-scripted literacy program with a paced schedule. Whole class read-alouds became less common as the basal reader, with simplified versions of stories or nonfiction accounts, became the primary reading material used in class. Leveled readers, or short stories with varying levels of linguistic complexity, were also used in small-group instruction. Students were increasingly assessed on their reading progress, which focused on fluent decoding, text-based comprehension, and higher-level comprehension such as prediction making. This changing curriculum narrowed school-sanctioned understandings of what counted as literacy practices.

The new principal also enacted an English-only homework policy. Yet, even with top-down directives, teachers found ways to shape the language ideologies, or beliefs about languages and their speakers, through their classroom and homework practices. Previously, teachers had worked with the bilingual migrant education coordinator and university students to translate homework schedules and instructions into Spanish. The new principal, a Latina immigrant herself who had worked with more bilingual parent populations, justified her English-only homework decision by claiming that parents should have to learn and use English. Such ideological beliefs about languages and language learning overlooked the limited opportunities that new immigrants had to learn English, despite their strong desire to do so (Worthy, 2006). Many teachers disregarded the English-only homework directive and continued to quietly send instructions in Spanish.

Although there was no official language policy for school-based learning, and over half of the students' families were Spanish dominant, English was undeniably assumed to be the language of schooling. Still, there was always wiggle room, and teachers, who were predominantly monolingual English speakers, often served as de facto language policymakers based on their choices of what languages to recognize and accept in their classrooms. Teachers' beliefs about languages and their belonging in schools mattered, and although there were no bilingual education programs for elementary students in Marshall, most teachers sought out ways to try to position Spanish as a resource upon which students could draw for learning.

CRISTIÁN'S ENGAGEMENT IN EMILY'S SCHOOLING

This section shows how Emily's father supported her education, as well as integrated important authentic language and literacy strategies that were not recognized or built upon within Grant's literacy curriculum. If recognized, these practices could be leveraged to better support bilingual students' literacy development at school.

Expanding Beyond Traditional School-Based Literacy Practices

Cristián regularly attended Emily's parent–teacher conferences, volunteered to chaperone fieldtrips, and saw himself as being engaged in Emily's schooling. Yet many of his language and literacy engagement practices differed from those recognized and valued within Emily's school. When talking about her literacy practices at home, Emily shared, "I read books with my mom a lot. Because my dad doesn't know how to read yet. Like, he doesn't know how to say them in—he knows how to read but not like saying it in a story. . . . He has never ever read to me. I think that he's afraid. Or he gets stuck in a word that he doesn't know." It is not surprising that when Emily thought about home-based literacy practices, she oriented to the quintessential White middle-class practice of storybook reading, which is often understood as the primary way that families support their young children's literacy development (Heath, 1983; Orellana & D'warte, 2010). Despite the diminishing presence of authentic teacher–student read-alouds in classrooms under assessment-oriented curricula, the high value placed on story reading at home was reinforced at each parent–teacher conference. Caregivers were reminded to read nightly with their child, handouts were distributed that offered tips for effective reading, and students were rewarded for their completion of reading logs.

Families varied greatly in their comfort and engagement with reading books aloud. Some, such as Martina's family, made sure it was a regular practice, and others—such as Cristián, Julio, and Mateo—proactively resisted these unfamiliar literacy practices. For Cristián, storybooks, especially in English, had not been part of his upbringing. He also avoided the emergent literacy flashcards and worksheets that focused on discrete print-based skills, often relying on other family members or friends' children to help Emily with these tasks. If evaluated based on restrictive definitions of school-sanctioned literacy practices, Cristián would be seen as uninvolved in his daughter's literacy development.

Una Buena Educación: A Good Education

In fact, Cristián was not uninvolved at all. His literacy pedagogies were reflective of *una buena educación*. He talked about his responsibilities to *educar* (educate) Emily, and when I asked if "educate" referred to academics, he explained:

> No . . . personally. In academics, we [her parents] can't teach Emily anything. Practically nothing. Why? Because I studied until 6th grade. Nothing more. Practically they taught us to read. Count. Divide. Add. A little about Mexican history. . . . Academically, we can't teach them [our kids] much. We can't teach them much because we didn't have an intensive academic education. No, no, no. Personally, I teach her about life. About herself as a person. About how her personality must be. I can teach her all about this. To respect and value. . . . That's what I teach her. Nothing else. Because I think that's where I can help her.

Cristián's orientation to *una buena educación* is common among families of Mexican heritage, and the way these beliefs are reflected in daily practices unfolds in dynamic ways (Arzubiaga & Adair, 2010; Valdés, 1996; Valenzuela, 1999). As Cristián highlights, *educación* (education) is not about academic prowess—instead, it centers on respect, moral values, loyalty to family, and acting politely and appropriately. Families' engagement practices, undergirded by notions of *una buena educación,* sometimes overlap with school-sanctioned practices, and at other times, they are more implicit forms of teaching and learning that fall outside the purview of school-sanctioned knowledge. For Cristián, one of the primary ways he instructed Emily was through explicit teaching and implicit modeling of linguistic appropriateness, which requires the development of metalinguistic awareness.

Pedagogies of the Home: Supporting Metalinguistic Awareness Through Teaching and Modeling of Linguistic Appropriateness

When I first met Cristián during Emily's kindergarten year, our interactions often occurred at school-based events, and the way he spoke in English and Spanish struck me as formal and professional. His clear and precise selection of lexical forms stood out to many of Grant's educators as well, so much so that they hoped to convince him to spearhead a new school-based Latin@ parents group because of his powerful oratory skills. Because I had the chance to get to know him across different contexts, I realized that this was just one of the many ways that he spoke, and I was impressed by his linguistic dexterity in both Spanish and English. Through his everyday interactions, he implicitly modeled appropriate ways with words across contexts and audiences. On social occasions, he was often the life of the party, similar to an unofficial MC as he energized partygoers with his jokes and enthusiasm. When hanging out with his brother-in-law, he would adapt a style of speech more common among young men from their small town. When speaking to a group comprised of Spanish and English monolinguals, he would translate his words into both languages. He implicitly demonstrated and could explicitly teach his understandings about languages.

Cristián also intentionally modeled his metalinguistic awareness and instructed his daughter to be proactive and knowledgeable about the words she used. He taught her to look for cognates of words that were similar in Spanish and English (such as *evaporarse* in Spanish and *evaporate* in English), and to use new words she encountered as an opportunity to ask what they meant. For instance, during one of Cristián's Sunday morning family breakfasts, Emily's parents discussed a friend who claimed to have five *fincas* in Mexico. Emily asked what a *finca* was and Cristián explained in Spanish that "a *finca* [estate] is a house with a great deal of land. It has farm houses, fields to plant crops, and many horses." Through this implicit language lesson, he did not provide a quick translation of the English equivalent, but instead sought out ways to continually develop Emily's Spanish repertoire and the contextual nuance needed to understand that a *finca*, in this case, was not simply a farm. In the following excerpt, he discussed Emily's use of the word *chido* (cool) without her knowing what it really meant, and he taught her to develop understandings about words and their appropriateness:

> After she said chido [cool], I turned around and I kept looking at her. And I said to her, "Honey, you don't know what that means. Don't say that word. Because you don't know. Maybe it's a bad word. And because you heard it you're going to say it? No, honey. Learn. Ask what it means. And if it is something that you can say, you'll say it. And learn when, how, and with whom you are going to say it."

Here, lessons about *buena educación* were clearly embedded in Cristián's educational conversation with his daughter. He was teaching her how to be respectful and appropriate across contexts, with specific attention to audience and purpose. Within her classroom, such abilities could be connected to literacy standards that ask students to tailor messages to specific audiences and purposes.

Buena educación was also tied to the purpose of developing metalinguistic awareness, or an overt understanding of how language works. As Kathy Escamilla and colleagues (2014) emphasize, children will be more successful academically if they "develop an understanding of and ability to talk about languages both within and across language systems" (p. 21). *Meta* means "about," and requires moving from implicit understandings of language use to being able to provide explicit explanations of how languages work. For bilingual children, it is particularly important to develop understandings of how the multiple languages in their repertoire (for example, Spanish and English) are similar and different so that they can leverage their knowledge across both languages to express meanings (Escamilla et al., 2014; Martínez, Orellana, Pacheco, & Carbone, 2008). For example, Cristián noticed how Emily would invert the adjective and noun order when speaking in Spanish, a common challenge for English–Spanish bilingual speakers because of the syntactical differences between the two languages (the order in English is adjective then noun, whereas in Spanish it is noun and then adjective). When he noticed that Emily would incorrectly say, "*una chiquita niña*" (a little girl) instead of the correct order for Spanish—"*una niña chiquita*" (a girl little)—he drew her attention to the different syntactical patterns in Spanish and English so that she could begin to notice and use the appropriate order. Through everyday educational interactions, he taught Emily to recognize cross-linguistic relationships, an important strategy to support her language and literacy development in English and Spanish.

Cristián also encouraged Emily to draw upon her knowledge in English and Spanish for learning. As many scholars have shown, students are more academically successful if they view both languages as resources that can help them, rather than as impediments that must be forgotten because they are confusing or do not count in their English medium schooling (Escamilla et al., 2014). In literacy development, students who use their knowledge of both languages to decode and comprehend their school-based readings in English, and who stop to figure out unfamiliar words rather than skipping over them, are more successful readers (Jiménez, García, & Pearson, 1995). Indeed, this is what Emily's father taught her to do when she encountered key new words. Teachers at Grant Elementary were intentional about teaching literacy strategies, such as using context cues, having students ask themselves if what they read or wrote made sense, and looking for familiar lexical portions within an English word to determine its meaning (such as recognizing *friend* in the word *unfriendly*). Yet these strategies did not explicitly include developing students' metalinguistic awareness, or ways that their knowledge of language and the relationships *among their languages* could be used to better understand school-based texts.

It is important to emphasize that teachers themselves do not have to be fluent in students' additional languages to incorporate metalinguistic strategies into their classrooms. Educators could learn a few cognates and model this strategy, such as recognizing that the English word *lunar* includes the Spanish word *luna*, meaning "moon." It is important to develop these literacy skills because bilingual children do not always inherently know how to recognize cognates. Students who are taught this approach, and have it supported in their classrooms through anchor charts or cognate hunts, are better able to leverage their resources from both languages to complete school-based tasks (Escamilla et al., 2014). Once teachers have sanctioned this practice, they can have students serve as experts who recognize and teach others about the cognates they find.

In addition to drawing upon cognates with her peers, Emily also incorporated her father's pedagogical strategy of linguistic appropriateness during school-based learning. One day, Emily, Abi, and Ben were asked to help a new student, Nhi, find a library book. Nhi was from Vietnam and was the only non-Spanish speaking immigrant student in the school. Ben and Abi began playfully using their rulers to tap each other, which Nhi began doing as well. Each time Ben said something to Nhi in English or Spanish, which Nhi could not understand, he would begin to laugh. Emily literally echoed her father as she told them in Spanish, "You see. Anything we do, she'll do. It's a single word. Maybe the words you said might be bad for her. You have to think about this before anything, because what if what we say to her, in her country, is bad? Or that we're laughing at her? The things that we said, maybe for her it's a bad word."

Emily clearly displayed an orientation to *buena educación*, of acting and speaking appropriately and kindly, in this school-based interaction. Although there was an expectation for students to be well behaved at school, it was also accepted that students may be playfully mischievous when not under teachers' direct observation. Emily, however, oriented to a firmer model of *buena educación* in which she stressed that students had a moral responsibility to be models for their new peer, even when they were outside of the teachers' gaze. Here, she helped foster a learning space in which she and her immigrant peers could be *bien educado* (well educated), and thus take on identities of belonging as students who were "worthy, valuable, and valued" (Arzubiaga & Adair, 2010, p. 306). In addition, she embedded aspects of her father's lessons on metalinguistic awareness. She demonstrated her awareness through overt explanations of how the linguistic choices they made could mean different things for different audiences, and that what they said could accidently be offensive to their new classmate from Vietnam.

If recognized and leveraged, such language and literacy practices hold potential for her school-based literacy instruction. For instance, within the classroom these strategies could be tied to inference making and character analysis. Emily used evidence from their interactions with Nhi (play hitting) and made an inference about the type of student Nhi would want to be (a well-behaved one). She then made conscious decisions regarding their language choices so that they would be appropriate for their audience and purpose—talking with their new friend Nhi. To build these connections to the school literacy curriculum, teachers have to proactively look to learn from families' and students' literacy practices.

ENVISIONING HUMANIZING FAMILY ENGAGEMENT:
TEACHERS AS LEARNERS

As part of humanizing family engagement, teachers could benefit by learning from immigrant families' language and literacy approaches and seek out ways to incorporate these pedagogies into their school-based literacy instruction. To do this, educators should take on the role of learners, not just experts. This requires understanding fathers like Cristián as "Supperdaddys" who engage in valuable language and literacy practices rather than dismissing their educative potential because of their limited formal schooling, national origin, language proficiencies, gender, or documentation status.

Focusing on the literacy resources that fathers bring to their children's learning raises important questions about school-based literacy instruction for bilingual children. Fathers like Cristián develop key language and literacy strategies, yet to fully benefit from these resources, educators should design and implement classroom-based instruction that fosters opportunities for children to tap into and leverage these resources for their school-based learning. Such an approach moves away from a one-size-fits-all literacy program to approach literacy instruction flexibly instead, with the teacher as a learner. The focus is not on discrete skills: Rather, the teacher first seeks to understand the resources a child brings to his or her reading and writing experiences and then determines the optimal approaches to build upon, and expand, the child's resources to navigate a range of texts for a range of purposes (Orellana & D'warte, 2010).

For Emily and many other students, their caregivers understood schooling through a lens of *una buena education*, which also encompassed the development of metalinguistic awareness so that they would make intentional language choices that were appropriate across contexts. Through the development of this literacy strategy, students like Emily were better equipped to critically draw upon their range of language and literacy resources in Spanish and English as they interacted, wrote, and read. They came to view their resources in Spanish as beneficial, rather than as a problem (the latter often being the underlying message of English medium schooling). Schooling that frames students as English language learners (ELLs) or limited English proficient (LEP), rather than as bilinguals in the making, does not position students' bilingual language and literacy practices as resources. Nonetheless, teachers can seek out ways to push against these deficit orientations to students' language and literacy practices by recognizing and building upon a wider range of literacy practices within their classrooms.

How to Learn from Families' Bilingual
Language and Literacy Practices

It is helpful to consider how educators can begin to learn from students' and families' home-based literacy practices. One way to achieve this is by looking closely at how children use language and literacy. Alim (2010) provides a comprehensive framework for how students themselves can begin to develop critical language awareness, or an understanding of how they use language and how language is sometimes used against them. This framework places students in the role of qualitative researcher, in which they keep journals, conduct interviews with family members, and analyze the ways languages are used appropriately across contexts in their daily lives. Because many of the language and literacy strategies that minoritized students draw upon may not be overtly obvious when asked, "What are your home-based literacy strategies?" Alim's framework could be adapted to help students foster an awareness of the literacy strategies they are already bringing to their learning and how these can be tailored to school-based literacy goals.

A second way to meet school-based literacy goals through families' home-based literacy practices is by integrating the development of metalinguistic awareness into the literacy curriculum. Although the development of metalinguistic awareness is rarely incorporated into conventional literacy goals in English medium schooling, literacy scholars in the field of bilingual education emphasize the salience of this strategy for all students who live and learn in two languages (Escamilla et al., 2014). This includes bilingual children, such as those profiled in this book who speak nondominant languages at home and attend English medium schooling. By developing their metalinguistic awareness, students can more effectively make connections across their language systems and draw upon their breadth of resources to transfer content knowledge and literacy strategies.

To illustrate how family-based literacy practices can be incorporated into the classroom, I present a typical lesson from Emily's 2nd-grade classroom, and then make suggestions for how it could be adapted to further develop Emily's home-based language and literacy practices. One afternoon, Mrs. Drescher previewed the story "At Play: Long Ago and Today" from the students' basal reader. She asked students the genre (an informational text), explained the comprehension strategy (determining the author's purpose), and highlighted the focal skill (readers asking themselves questions to better understand what they are reading). She then engaged students in a phonics lesson on the /y/ and /ey/ sounds before explaining the use of possessives, which she described as "something that is mine or belongs to me." She defined the eight key vocabulary words from the story and then introduced the eight high-frequency sight words (for example, *of*, *here*) that students had to memorize. One student commented on the silent *e* in a word, drawing upon a previous phonics lesson, and Mrs. Drescher highlighted that this is what good students do: They actively take information from one lesson and look for ways to connect it to others; they make connections.

There are several ways within this lesson that Mrs. Drescher could incorporate and expand the language and literacy strategies that Cristián taught Emily. For instance, she could highlight cross-linguistic connections by having students draw upon their knowledge of Spanish cognates to understand the vocabulary. Indeed, five of the eight vocabulary words had close cognates in Spanish (*nominate—nominar, recreation—recreación, recently—recientemente, archaic—arcaico, official—oficial*). Although it is possible students may not know the meanings of these words in Spanish, terms they did know could help them better understand and remember the English vocabulary terms and comprehend the story.

Like Cristián's explanations of adjective order, in Mrs. Drescher's lesson on possessives, she could draw attention to differences in the structures of English and Spanish, such as the common use of an apostrophe in English, compared with the use of the word *de* (of) in Spanish (for instance, Emily's house versus *la casa de Emily* [the house of Emily]). Mrs. Drescher was not a Spanish speaker, but she could look up key differences between Spanish and English online or through language comparison tables (see Shatz & Wilkinson, 2013, for tables of the six most common languages in U.S. schools). Finally, when encouraging students to make connections, she could explain how strategies they bring to their learning don't only come from other school-based lessons, as she implied in the phonics example. They can also come from the ways that students learn to use language and literacy at home. By explicitly naming students' home-based literacy strategies in Spanish and English as resources, creating visual spaces where they become sanctioned (such as through cognate anchor charts), and bringing bilingual books into classroom libraries, teachers can incorporate and expand students' knowledges about language and literacy to meet academic goals.

It is important to recognize that teachers do not have to be bilingual themselves to welcome and build upon these literacy practices in their classrooms. When educators come to understand themselves as expert in some things, but learners in others, they can open up spaces for students, families, and community members to authentically partner in children's language and literacy development. Teachers' school-based literacy instruction can proactively draw upon and leverage the range of multilingual resources that students bring to their school-based learning.

PEDAGOGICAL TAKEAWAYS

- Conventional approaches to literacy, which emphasize the isolated development of literacy skills, offer a single, restrictive approach to literacy that does not align with most immigrant families' literacy practices and strategies.
- Incorporating metalinguistic awareness is useful for all students, especially those who live in more than one language. Some ways to do this include:
  - ➤ creating cognate or false-cognate anchor charts, in which students learn to search for similar words across their languages (Escamilla et al., 2014);

> ➤ learning about the basic structures of languages students speak, which would help teachers understand how students are using knowledge from their home language (Shatz & Wilkinson, 2013);
> ➤ engaging students in a unit on developing their critical language awareness, modeled after Alim (2010), in which students research the ways that language and literacy are used in their homes and communities; and
> ➤ remembering that educators do not need to be bilingual themselves, or teach in bilingual schools, to incorporate these approaches.
> • Some families do engage in storybook reading, and appreciate the inclusion of bilingual storybooks for their children to bring home.
> ➤ If bilingual books are not available, work with bilingual college students or design a family event in which English storybooks become bilingual by writing the text in an additional language.
> ➤ Websites (such as http://www.colorincolorado.org) offer useful resources to work with emergent bilingual students and their families around literacy.

REFLECTION QUESTIONS

1. What is literacy for you? Reading? Writing?
   a. What types of reading and writing practices do your definitions help you recognize?
   b. What types of practices do your definitions cause you to overlook?
2. If Emily were your student, how would you seek out ways to recognize and incorporate her home-based language and literacy practices in Spanish and English into your classroom literacy curriculum?
3. What language ideologies and unofficial language policies exist in your school or classroom? How might you open up spaces to value students' additional languages and tap into them for school-based goals?

WORKING WITH IMMIGRANT AND UNDOCUMENTED FAMILIES

Chapter 5

Reading the Word and Reading the World as Undocumented Immigrants

Abi and Mateo's Diverse Literacy Practices

As Abi opened the door to let me into her family's apartment, she asked her father if she was allowed to tell me what had happened. He responded yes, and Abi explained that she had not been in school today because *la migra* (immigration officers) had come to their home and threatened to take her father away, but did not. Her family could not share more details because her parents were on their way to work. They explained that everything was fine, and we arranged to talk more the next day.

This chapter explores her father's language and literacy-based pedagogies of the home, expanding on those relayed in Chapter 3, to address the question "What counts as literacy?" Through looking at a story Mateo and Abi co-narrate about police coming to their home and examining translation practices and the impact of documentation status, the chapter shows how fathers like Mateo prepare their children to read both the word and the world. Mateo's home-based literacy practices were reflective of Freirean (1970, 2001) literacy approaches that emphasize teaching minoritized students to read the *word* through the development of literacy skills while also developing their abilities to read the *world* by reflecting on their political context. Mateo taught Abi about reading the word by developing her oracy skills, or the language needed to engage with texts, through storytelling, riddles, and translation. He taught her to read the world by preparing her to safely navigate her surroundings as a member of an undocumented family. These forms of language and literacy development were not recognized or built upon within Abi's schooling. Yet, within a context where undocumented immigrants' belonging and language resources are regularly questioned, educators should learn from these expanded literacy practices and foster school-based language and literacy pedagogies that prepare children to read both the word and the world.

THE POLITICAL CONTEXT OF UNDOCUMENTED FAMILIES

The Criminalization of Undocumented Immigrants

Mateo and Abi lived in a political context in which undocumented immigrants were increasingly targeted and deported for minor infractions. Prior to 2009, a person's undocumented status would lead to deportation if the person committed a serious crime or was stopped by an immigration officer. Federal immigration programs such as Secure Communities and the Immigration and Nationality Act, Section 287(g), changed the day-to-day landscape for undocumented immigrants, and under the Obama administration deportations reached unprecedented levels. These types of programs deputized local police officers as immigration officials, permitting them (and often requiring them) to pass along an individual's information to immigration authorities if officers suspected that a person may not have U.S. documentation. Although these immigration programs claimed to target dangerous criminals, in reality they led to the mass deportation of many low-level offenders without criminal histories, such as those who committed traffic violations (Kohli, Markowitz, & Chavez, 2011). Within a context of unprecedented deportations, families had to negotiate the potential deportation of their loved ones as well as morality-laden public debates regarding undocumented immigrants in which their integrity and belonging were regularly questioned (Chávez, 2008).

During the height of these programs in Marshall in 2011, many Latino immigrant men were deported for minor infractions such as driving without a Pennsylvania license. The precariousness of this situation is important to understand: In most states, undocumented immigrants do not have a pathway to obtain a valid U.S. driver's license, but driving is a regular necessity for most families. Thus, each time they drive (for example, to a parent–teacher conference, to work, and so forth), they are in danger of being pulled over, which could lead to deportation. The "crime" they have committed is driving without a valid U.S. driver's license, which they cannot obtain. Most parents without documentation were painstakingly careful drivers, and the instant their children saw a police cruiser they would freeze to avoid drawing attention from officers. Mateo taught 7-year-old Abi these important ways of reading the world through everyday educational conversations. For instance, one Saturday as I drove Abi's family to run errands, she asked me if I was scared of the police. Mateo intervened in a soft voice and explained that unlike the adults in Abi's family, I was able to get a driver's license. If police officers stopped me for an infraction I might have to pay a fine, but they would not send me away. Brief lessons like these taught Abi about the unequal treatment undocumented immigrants experienced and prepared her for high-stakes interactions with police authorities, such as the interaction described below.

Police Officers Coming to the Door: Mateo and Abi's Narrative

I returned to Abi's home the day after she told me about *la migra* (immigration) coming to their door, and Mateo clarified that they had been police officers, not immigration. Bachata music played in the background as Mateo, Abi, her baby brother, and I sat down to the dinner Mateo had prepared. I mentioned how I had heard recently about local police officers going to Latin@ families' homes and insisting that they be let in. Once inside, police officers would ask for household members' *papeles* (immigration papers) to prove that they had official documentation to reside in the United States. It was rumored that police officers then passed along this information to immigration authorities, and many adult Latino males were taken into custody. The "crime" that led to immigrants' detainment, in many cases, was not having U.S. documentation. I told Mateo and Abi how I had worried this was what had happened to them. They explained that they were lucky, because the police did not ask for their papers. They shared the following story about two sets of police officers who insisted on entering without a warrant, or the kinds of official "papers" police needed to cross the border into people's homes.

> *Mateo:* We were waiting for Viviana's [a friend's] dad to take Abi to school. And I was there, standing at the window, to see when he arrived. Suddenly a car passed by. And, well, the police had come. They were looking toward the house and they parked. And I saw that they were coming here. And I told Abi, "I bet they're from Immigration." Haha. I said, "Don't go and open the door." And yes. They arrived and knocked. They asked us a question—ah no—they told us to open the door. And I said to Abi, "Ay, Abi. Ask them what they want." She asked them and they didn't tell her anything. Just that they were the police and that we should open the door. I said, "What do they want?"
>
> *Abi:* He [the officer] said, "I'm the police. Open the door." Right, Dad?
>
> *Sarah:* But did they have a police car?
>
> *Abi:* Uh-huh. And then when they leave, when I tell them, "Why you didn't show our papers[1] [warrant]?" They said, "I'm the police, open the door." I said, "My dad said that where's the papers [warrant] and where's everything."
>
> *Mateo:* They needed a paper [warrant] to have us open up. And no. They didn't do anything. Better that they leave. Done. From there everything was fine then. Afterwards another police came at like—
>
> *Sarah:* Another one came?
>
> *Mateo:* Later. Much later. Like at 12. Two hours later.
>
> *Sarah:* And did they go to a lot of people's houses, or just your house?
>
> *Mateo:* Just ours.
>
> *Abi:* Just this one. They knocked on the middle apartment door [of the

building] first, then the one upstairs, then the one downstairs.

Sarah: Hmm. And do you think they stopped because they saw in the window? Or because someone—

Mateo: No. I'll tell you what happened.

Abi: And Dad. But when I said, "Can you show your papers [warrant]?" He said, "What's going on there?" . . .

Mateo: Yeah. But the other police came later.

Abi: He [an officer] said to me. He said, "What's going on in there?"

Sarah: The other police arrived?

Mateo: Um-hm. The same thing. The police came to the door. And I told her [Abi] to ask what it is that they wanted. Now this police told us, "Yes I'm looking for a person. Open the door. If not, I'll enter with force." And then I open the door for him. Once he sees me, he then grabs his radio and says, "No. It's not the same person." And they open up a paper with a picture of a person.

Sarah: A person from Mex—

Mateo: Hispanic. . . . So he asked me if I know him, or if he lives here. "Well, no," I said, "No. He doesn't live here." "Not upstairs?" "No." "Downstairs?" "No." "Okay. It's fine." "No problem."

Abi: And he left.

Sarah: He left?

Mateo: Haha. He asked Abi why she hadn't gone to school.

Sarah: Ha. And what did you say?

Abi: "No. It's because I got scared in the morning when you were knocking the door." And he said . . . and he said, "What?" "Because I thought that you were going to bring my dad to the police." . . .

Mateo: Let's see. In Spanish . . .

Abi: (translating into Spanish) He said, the police said why I hadn't gone to school. And I said because they [the police] scared me.

Reading the World: Developing Politicized Funds of Knowledge

Mateo and Abi's story about police officers and regular educative interactions regarding undocumented status illustrate how minoritized caregivers teach their young children to read the world. This is a form of literacy that prepares students to navigate and contest discrimination they may face as members of minoritized groups. Mateo developed Abi's funds of knowledge, or the historical and cultural bodies of knowledge cultivated within families and communities (Moll et al., 1992). As members of an undocumented family, this entailed recognizing what Holly Link and I (2015) have called *politicized funds of knowledge*. These are the real-world experiences, knowledges, and skills that young people use and develop across home and school contexts that are often positioned as taboo or unsafe to incorporate into classroom learning. For Latin@ immigrant students, politicized funds of knowledge may include the knowledges they learn through navigating citizenship status, engaging in transgressive bilingual language play (Martínez & Morales, 2014), or writing poetry about border crossing. By explicitly naming these as politicized funds of knowledge, I hope to bring attention to a range of experiences that are often excluded from schooling and to unpack the challenges and potential of incorporating them within classrooms. Although challenging, this is particularly important within contexts of anti-immigrant sentiment and heightened discrimination against diverse students.

Through her engagement in this difficult incident, Abi gained insights into important politicized funds of knowledge. She learned about the dangers of being a Mexican-looking man standing near the window of your own home, as this was enough for police officers to pull over and knock on your door. She learned not to open the door for police officers, if possible, and that police officers should have a warrant to lawfully enter your home. She also learned that police officers do not always follow these rules. She learned the importance of navigating when to draw upon the right to remain silent and when to speak up to disrupt injustices. For example, Abi's responses to the police officer's question about missing school illustrate the agentive and tactful ways she had learned to read the world and engage with authority figures. Rather than remaining silent, Abi named how she was scared that they were going to take her dad away. By explaining that her absence from school was the result of fear instilled by police officers rather than apathy toward her schooling, she debunked myths about Latin@s' indifference toward schooling. Through her retelling of these experiences with her father, she also engaged in an act of reclaiming their home as a safe space, one that should remain free from police vigilance.

This interaction also points to the powerful ways children engage with and make sense of documentation status in their daily lives. Many scholars argue that children's awareness of documentation status does not become concretely understood until they face overt structural discrimination, such as adolescents who cannot apply for driver's licenses or college financial aid (Gonzales, 2011). Abi, even as a 6-year-old, was routinely grappling with subtle messages about documentation status available during routine activities, such as her questions about my driver's license. Caregivers are keenly aware of the necessity to develop their children's abilities to read the world so that they can safely navigate their schools and communities as members of undocumented families (Arango, Flores, Gallo, Lara, Link, Arreguín, & Peregrina, 2016).

Like most teachers in the early grades at Grant Elementary, Abi's teacher had limited awareness about local deportation practices or their effects on students. In conversations about why she and many other students didn't share their immigration experiences with teachers, Abi highlighted that she "didn't have enough *confianza* in them to tell them anything." Abi felt that teachers shied away from the more politicized funds of knowledge students brought to school as Mexican immigrants, which Abi took as a message that these experiences were not safe or welcome in the classroom. It was with her father that

Abi developing funds of knowledge about local deportation practices, in part to protect herself from being the target of these discriminatory practices. Yet, for Abi and many immigrant children, these resources went unnoticed in school.

PEDAGOGIES OF THE HOME: STORYTELLING AND TRANSLATION

Developing Oracy Through Storytelling and Double Meanings

Storytelling was a regular part of Mateo and Abi's home-based language and literacy practices. It was common for Mateo to implicitly model engaging storytelling to his daughter, provide explicit feedback on her stories when the details lacked coherence, or to feign falling asleep mid-story if she was not engaging her listeners. The value placed on high-quality storytelling was evident in this police narrative. Abi and Mateo drew upon key narrative devices that are valued in school-based literacy, such as sequenced events with important details, quoted speech and physical gestures to build characters and engage listeners, and a clear ending that answered the question why Abi had not attended school the previous day (see Gallo, 2016, for a full analysis). Many of these devices were also evident in Abi's oral narratives, as illustrated in this short excerpt from a 30-minute story she told me about crossing the border:

> Then we all formed one line, haha, and I was laughing so much, I had to stay like this (acts out arms straight down). "Very firm, march!" they said. . . . We crossed again. Immigration didn't find us. . . . Well, yeah, there was Immigration, only we had to jump around to the other side. But there it wasn't very easy. It was harder. We had to rip our pants—rip this part, and this part. Because they said they could get caught on something that was in our pockets. . . . So we hopped up and when the lights [from border patrol] shined on us, we had to grab a stick like this, and they couldn't see us [the lights would flash below their feet]. Because of the light, we had to hang there. Hanging! They held me from here (pointing to her waist), and I held myself up from the stick. Haha. It was very hard because my mom couldn't sustain me a whole lot. I was 4 years old, but I was very heavy.

Abi told a sequenced narrative during this border crossing story. In the previous portions (not included here), she explained how she and her mother first flew to the Mexican border, and then attempted to cross, unsuccessfully, twice. In this excerpt, she shared their third attempt at crossing, which was successful. In subsequent portions (also not included), she then explained their journey from the border to Pennsylvania, where she met her father for the first time. In this excerpt and throughout the narrative, she included important details and built characters, such as a malevolent human smuggler she called *el gato* (the cat) because he used to scratch on the door before entering the apartment where they hid near the border. Her inclusion of gestures and quoted speech engaged her listener, such as her laughter-filled descriptions of having to march in a silent line so as not to be detected by the border patrol. Her narrative was full of suspense (crossing three times), included overcoming difficult physical feats (hanging from a stick), and took stances on characters who were good (Abi, her mom) and bad (*el gato*). The politicized funds of knowledge that she developed from crossing the border are evident in this story. Here, and in many of her collaborative narratives with her father, Abi also developed important literacy skills related to oracy.

Oracy is the language needed to interact with texts. As Escamilla and colleagues (2014) explain, oracy "is an aspect of oral language, but it includes a *more specific subset* of skills and strategies within oral language that more closely relates to literacy objectives in academic settings" (p. 21, italics in original). Activities that help develop students' oracy include storytelling, dramatizations, interviews, riddles, jokes, tongue-twisters, rhymes, and songs. These activities were a regular part of Mateo's home-based pedagogies. These literacy pedagogies are perhaps not surprising because of the strong emphasis on verbal artistry found in many Mexican communities (Guerra, 1998) and the value placed on the relationship between oral language skills and literacy development in the Mexican National Reading Program. In the United States, however, the conventional skills approach that dominates early literacy instruction today (see Chapter 4) minimizes the importance of developing these interactive oral language skills. This is despite research such as the National Literacy Panel (August & Shanahan, 2006) that has shown the key role that oral language development plays in English literacy development for all students, and especially nonnative English speakers. In contrast to the conventional approach to literacy instruction in most public schools today, Escamilla and colleagues (2014) suggest that a quarter of literacy instruction should be dedicated to developing students' oracy.

In addition to storytelling development, Mateo developed Abi's oracy by teaching her to recognize and creatively play with *el doble sentido*, or double meanings, of words. At home, Mateo often included humorous double meanings in his talk that were meant to playfully tease his audience (Martínez & Morales, 2014). Sometimes they were simple sayings such as "*Es una comida que pica, pero no le pica*" (A food that is spicy, but it doesn't bite). Sometimes they included bilingual language play, such as "oh my *gatos*" (oh my cats) instead of "oh my god"—taking advantage of the parallel sounds of "ga" in Spanish and /go/ sound in the world *god*. He also manipulated the sounds in words to playfully poke fun at people, such as saying "*sancho*" rather than "*salud*" when someone sneezed. This was a play on words that referenced a spouse's lover and thus insinuated that the person who sneezed was being cheated on. I admittedly had a difficult time following Mateo's regular creative displays, and Abi often took on the role of interpreter, warning me not to answer him because he might try to catch me in a trap or explaining the multiple meanings of the words he was using.

Abi could overtly explain how her father was using oral Spanish language and paid great attention to the form of words. By 2nd grade, Abi began to talk about the "*dos formas*" (two forms) of many different words. Similar to her explanations of her dad's double meanings, she would often stop peers in school to explain how words like *circo* in Spanish could mean "circuit" or "circus" in English. She predominantly demonstrated this awareness in Spanish and enjoyed taking on the role of the classroom Spanish expert within peer-based interactions. In contrast, students' expertise in Spanish was rarely called upon during teacher-fronted lessons. Abi began applying this strategy to English as well, such as her realization of the different meanings for the words *girl* and *friend* and *girlfriend*. And although she and her father regularly exploited sounds in Spanish when engaging in this oral language play (such as "*sa-ncho*" instead of "*sa-lud*"), Abi was never instructed in how to transfer this skill to phonemic awareness development in English.

Within the police story, Mateo and Abi played with the double meaning of the word *papeles*, meaning "papers." Immigrant families usually talked about papers as the official documents people needed to reside in the United States. Here, Mateo and Abi used the *doble sentido* of the same word, *papers*, to reference a warrant, or the official documentation that police officers needed to enter their home. Rather than viewing undocumented immigrants as unlawful or morally questionable, by playing with the meaning of the word *papers*, Mateo and Abi were able to position the police officers as unreasonable and unlawful for forcibly entering their home without a warrant. Although this was a subtle move, it created a way for Abi to push back against the prevailing deficit messages in the media that claimed undocumented immigrants were illegal and immoral. Instead, she and Mateo named the police officers as the ones crossing the border into the sanctity of their home, without the legal document they were supposed to possess. In this case, Abi was developing the tools she needed to see herself as valuable, reasonable, and belonging within a context that often sent messages that undocumented immigrants were not welcome.

In this story, Mateo also used humor to bring levity to a serious topic, which helped lessen some of the deep pain associated with the term *papeles*. Although *papers* was just a word, it created material consequences for their family, such as the years they had been divided by borders during Abi's early childhood because they lacked the official documentation to visit one another in Mexico and the United States. As shown during her border-crossing story, Abi, too, drew upon humor to find ways to broach the difficult topics related to undocumented status. In addition, a few weeks after the police story, she walked up to the locked door of their apartment, knocked briskly, and shouted in a deep voice, "It's the police." She then broke out into uncontrollable laughter as her parents opened the door. By doing this, she used humor as a release and as a strategy to bring up the police incident that was clearly on her mind. Like her father, she used humor to make a topic that she sincerely worried about speakable and to break through silences that caused her fear and pain.

Translation and School-Based Literacy

In the incident with the police officers Abi also served as a translator between her father and the police. Like most children of immigrants in Marshall, Abi took on the role as translator across contexts such as school, stores, and home. Translation was often a collaborative language practice, in which children and adults drew upon their ranges of linguistic and cultural knowledge to successfully complete real-world tasks. Here, Abi drew upon her developing resources in English and Spanish to communicate with the police officers, and her father contributed important legal information, such as their need to show a warrant. Mateo fostered opportunities for Abi to continually develop her translation skills, such as his request that she translate the police officer's message about school into Spanish at the end of this story. In Marshall, children shared in interviews that translating was important, enjoyable, and beneficial for them, their families, and the community. Children were not just supporting their families who were not fluent in English; they were also helping teachers, store clerks, medical staff, and police officers who were not fluent in Spanish—although the United States is the world's second largest Spanish-speaking country. As Marjorie Faulstich Orellana (2009) details, despite ideologies in the United States that position children's translation practices as detrimental, translation is a cognitively beneficial and emotionally satisfying process.

However, in certain cases, children can also be racialized when engaging in translation, and Abi did not like translating during high-stakes encounters such as this one with the police. In this interaction, Abi was aware of the ways that the police officers assumed her family was doing something wrong because of their questions such as "What's goin' on in there?" This question gave the impression that behind their closed apartment door, Abi and her father were engaged in deviant behavior, rather than simply getting ready for school. Although translating during such stressful encounters was rare, such situations understandably caused Abi anxiety. Translating was a discursive practice, but it had real-world, material consequences for her and her family, such as the police potentially taking her father away if she said the wrong thing.

Abi's translation practices, despite the stressful nature of this rare interaction with police, highlight an untapped literacy resource that could be built upon in her schooling. Translation is a language practice that draws upon language strategies similar to those needed to decipher written texts. While translating, Abi had to shift voices and carefully navigate the presentation of other speakers' words so that they were appropriately presented for each audience. For instance, in another portion of their retelling, Abi softened her father's more direct question, "Where are the papers?" to "Can you show your papers?" when she translated the message to the police officers. When developing as writers, students need to learn to shift voices as they write from various perspectives and for different audiences.

Many students from immigrant families have experience as translators, and these language practices can enhance their school literacy development (Durán, 2016; Martínez et al., 2008; Orellana, 2009). This can be accomplished by a literacy curriculum that validates these skills, builds critical language awareness regarding how students deploy them, and ties these strategies to literacy practices. Martínez et al. (2008) detail a literacy curriculum of this nature, and provide useful suggestions for educators who are interested in drawing upon students' translation practices for academic writing. They encourage educators to validate students' translating practices through whole class discussions, student journals that track these experiences, and invitations to students to bring in sample texts they have translated. They also illustrate how educators can help build students' metalinguistic awareness around their translation practices through reenactments of difficult translation situations, in which students collaboratively analyze the ways that they shifted voices for different audiences and purposes. To bridge these practices to academic writing, they suggest activities in which students practice writing persuasive texts for various audiences and engage in collaborative analyses to highlight how they utilized different grammar, argument structures, and vocabulary as they engaged in this writing, just as they do while translating. Like Abi's translation and literacy experiences with her father, throughout this curriculum Martínez and colleagues (2008) stress the importance of designing opportunities for collaborative and authentic literacy experiences.

Although Abi developed strong oracy skills in Spanish with her father at home, she did not have opportunities to pair these with Spanish reading and writing activities. There were no bilingual education programs for elementary school students in Marshall, and outside of home-based literacy practices Abi had no spaces to develop her Spanish literacy or oracy. In her English medium schooling at Grant Elementary, as a student who entered schooling without previous exposure to English, Abi did not excel in the isolated skills-based approach to early literacy. She could successfully engage in manipulating sounds when embedded in authentic word play in Spanish with her father, but in oral literacy practices with her father, changing the sounds had real-world purpose, such as playful teasing or the demonstration of wit through clever manipulations of words. School-based phonemic awareness exercises could be considered oracy development because they require students to isolate and manipulate sounds. However, school-sanctioned phonemic awareness drills in English lacked a meaningful context. They were also difficult for Abi because she was just beginning to develop her resources in English and could not remember the anchor words for each sound on her letter flashcards. When she looked at the picture of the monkey scratching to illustrate the /i/ sound in the word *itch*, a relatively obscure word in English that is very difficult to pronounce for Spanish speakers, she could not remember the word or think of the Spanish term, which did not begin with the /i/ sound. The isolated word and sound drills did not achieve any social purpose the way word play with her father did.

Authentic literacy experiences were important for Abi, and these were rare at school. Abi was part of the lowest-leveled literacy groups, which at times meant computer-based practice in literacy skills rather than teacher-based instruction. Her lively, detail filled stories in Spanish were inaccessible to her monolingual English-speaking teachers, and because assessments relied on the skills-based conceptions of emergent literacy in English, Abi was largely left to master these skills before she could try out other literacy practices. Yet, when Abi was given an opportunity for authentic writing, she became focused and engaged. For example, during a Valentine's Day celebration, she felt badly that most of her classmates had brought in treats and Valentines, and she had not because her family did not have the financial resources. As her classmates swarmed around her and ate candy, she sat glued in her chair, writing out a heartfelt Valentine in English to her teachers. It read, "I'm so sorry I didn't bring candy, but I'm givin' you a card," which Mrs. Drescher profoundly thanked her for. It is noteworthy that this authentic literacy practice occurred during a classroom celebration, outside of the official literacy curriculum.

Abi's teachers and father were deeply engaged in trying to teach her to read the word, but the lack of alignment across their approaches was too much for Abi to navigate on her own. Her father's literacy pedagogies were important—he knew he had to engage her in authentic practices and drew upon his verbal artistry to develop her oracy in Spanish and bilingual translation skills. But these were not paired with text-based literacy practices in Spanish at school or home. At school, Abi's literacy experiences were almost exclusively in English, focusing on discrete, code-based literacy skills and they rarely included the types of authentic literacy practices that engaged Abi. Abi came to see herself as an unskilled reader, and she lacked confidence when it came to engaging in school-sanctioned literacy practices.

ENVISIONING HUMANIZING FAMILY ENGAGEMENT: WHAT COUNTS AS LITERACY

Reading the Word and the World

This chapter has shown how one father taught his daughter to read the word and the world as a Spanish–English emergent bilingual from an undocumented family. These were not the literacy practices of Abi's school, and despite the positive humanizing relationship that Mateo established with Abi's teacher Mrs. Drescher (Chapter 3), the caring adults in her life were not successful in coming together to support Abi in reading the word. Her father's literacy pedagogies were not enough on their own, and the narrow, school-based approaches did not work for Abi. Abi represents the ways rigid English-only approaches to school-based literacy fail minoritized students by discounting the incredible language and literacy resources that they bring to school. It is important to consider that if a talented student like Abi struggles with literacy development in school, the problem is not with Abi, but with the approaches being used to teach literacy.

Bilingual Schooling to Read the Word and the World

Today, almost a quarter of public school students come from immigrant families and bring bilingual resources to their classrooms. Educational research has shown that bilingual children are most academically successful in their home language *and English* when they are enrolled in high-quality bilingual education programs (e.g., Escamilla et al., 2014; Thomas & Collier, 1997). However, such bilingual programs are rare in most parts of the United States. This is not because bilingual programs do not work but rather because some state laws have outlawed bilingual education, federal funding sources have prioritized English language acquisition over bilingual development, and assessment mandates have deeply constrained the ways bilingualism and biliteracy can be developed in school. Our current schooling approaches, which subtract the linguistic and literacy resources that bilingual children bring to school, are ideological—which also means they can change.

It is likely that Abi, if she could have attended a high-quality bilingual school, would have had the opportunity to develop text-based Spanish oracy and literacy skills that would have complemented her father's language and literacy pedagogies. A bilingual program would have been able to recognize and build upon Abi's many language and literacy resources and transfer her literacy abilities to English over time. However, many districts do not offer bilingual education programs. This means that teachers in English medium programs must also be prepared to recognize and draw from bilingual students' language and literacy resources. In this final section, I revisit the humanizing family engagement framework to explore how educators and families could foster more successful literacy experiences for students like Abi. To move toward humanizing family engagement, school-based literacy practices should expand what counts as literacy by building upon ways bilingual students from undocumented families successfully read the word and the world.

What Counts as Literacy

Like Cristián's lessons on metalinguistic awareness, the ways that Mateo taught Abi to read the word through oracy skills and translation were not recognized or built upon at school. Uncritically orienting to a conventional approach to literacy education is unlikely to best support Abi and many of her classmates,

as Latin@ bilingual students are not well served by most conventional literacy approaches (National Center for Education Statistics, 2013). Educators and
teacher educators would benefit from understanding the unique resources and
needs that bilingual students bring to their literacy practices. One way to do
this is by drawing upon literacy research, such as the synthesis conducted by
the National Literacy Panel (August & Shanahan, 2006), which places bilingual
students at the forefront of school literacy programs, rather than treating them
as an afterthought.

Mateo's lessons on reading the world helped Abi make sense of, cope with,
and subtly refashion the ways in which documentation status shaped her life in
a context of deportations. Rather than understanding these father–daughter interactions as simplistic storytelling or joking around, it is clear how Mateo's engaging Abi in important educational lessons about documentation status created
a mechanism for her to understand herself as a good, moral person against the
prevailing images of illegal immigrants who do not belong in the United States.
Mateo's pedagogies, like those of the other fathers in this book, offered children
lessons on how to examine critically and reshape the story of who they are. In a
context in which undocumented Latin@ immigrants' humanity and belonging
are regularly questioned, Mateo's positive educational development of ways to
read the world cannot be underestimated.

How to Expand What Counts as Literacy

It is useful to consider how Abi's teachers could have learned from Mateo's home-
based language and literacy practices to better support Abi's literacy development in her English medium school. They could achieve this by incorporating
several of the curricular suggestions from this chapter, such as a stronger emphasis on oracy within the literacy curriculum and teaching students to transfer
their oral literacy skills to writing. If Abi effectively developed these strategies in
one language, with supports she could also transfer them to Spanish and across
her languages (Escamilla et al., 2014). As educators who worked with predominantly bilingual Mexican immigrant and bidialectal African American students,
her teachers could also look for ways to adopt the translation literacy curriculum in their classrooms. Finally, they could seek out ways to incorporate more
authentic writing experiences. Based on Abi's Valentine writing and her fathers'
authentic engagement with language play and storytelling, Abi thrived when she
was provided with opportunities to write to real people for real reasons.

Abi's teachers could also provide ways for their students to engage in bilingual
literacy practices with their families. For instance, Durán (2016) describes how an
elementary school teacher incorporated bilingual message journals into her classroom literacy practices. Twice a week, students wrote to a suggested prompt and
then invited someone in their family to respond. Because most students were from
bilingual families, this opened up opportunities for biliteracy practices. In order to
develop students' metalinguistic awareness regarding their language choices and

how they switched voices for different audiences (such as their Spanish-dominant mother or English-dominant cousin), journal writing was supported by intentional conferencing and whole group analyses of their written exchanges. Finally, Durán (2016) emphasized that these journals do not have to occur in bilingual schools. The incorporation of literacy journals could foster literacy and biliteracy practices that build upon and expand students' home-based language and literacy practices to meet school-based literacy goals. Such literacy pedagogies would not only have drawn upon Abi's strengths, but also those of many of her classmates who came from bilingual and bidialectal families.

PEDAGOGICAL TAKEAWAYS

- Incorporate the development of students' oracy into your literacy curriculum (Escamilla et al., 2014). You can do this through storytelling, language play, and drama.
- If your curriculum permits, try out a literacy unit that centers on translation (e.g., Martínez et al., 2008).
  - ➤ Validate students' translation experiences and invite them to bring these spoken and written experiences into the classroom.
  - ➤ Build students' awareness of the ways they shift voices for different audiences and purposes as they translate.
  - ➤ Create authentic, collaborative writing activities in which students try out and analyze the ways they draw on similar strategies when they write for different audiences.
- Try incorporating family message journals or other collaborative bilingual writing assignments into your literacy curriculum (Durán, 2016).
- Integrate authentic literacy experiences, such as persuasive letters to local decisionmakers or a bilingual classroom newsletter, supported by bilingual university or community volunteers.
- Caregivers from minoritized backgrounds engage in important literacy pedagogies in which they teach their children to read the world, or safely navigate a society that unjustly discriminates against them.
  - ➤ Work with trusted colleagues to find ways to address, rather than avoid, controversial topics that are often silenced in the classroom. This work is even more important in contexts of heightened discrimination against student difference.
  - ➤ Example topics include undocumented status, racialization and Black Lives Matter movements, and the experiences of LGBTQ people and families.

REFLECTION QUESTIONS

---

1. What are your experiences and perspectives about children serving as translators? What ideologies do you think may shape your perspectives?
2. Think about the oracy and translation skills that Mateo developed at home. What are ways you could imagine building upon these skills within your classroom?
3. What are your experiences with bilingual education programs? How can you support bilingual education programs, even if you are not qualified to teach in them?
4. How do you open up spaces in your classroom for minoritized students to draw upon their experiences reading the world for their learning?
   a. What politicized funds of knowledge, or real-world experiences that are often positioned as taboo or unsafe to incorporate into classroom learning, do you think your students bring to your classroom?
   b. How might you open up safe spaces for students to talk or write about these experiences?
   c. What are the challenges of engaging in this during times of strong anti-immigrant sentiment or heightened discrimination? What are the consequences of not working against these silencing and discriminatory practices for minoritized students in your school?

Chapter 6

Undocumented Status and Elementary Schooling

> Shame shame.
> I don't want to go to Mexico
> No more more more.
> There's a big fat policeman
> At my door door door.
> He grabbed me by the collar.
> He made me pay a dollar.
> I don't want to go to Mex-i-co
> No more more—Shut the door!

Princess sang this rhyme when she was a 1st-grader, seated at her Barbie play table, as she took a break from her homework. This was a popular rhyme among students and represented the realities faced by many Latin@ immigrant children as new immigration policies led to increased parental deportations in Marshall. In this chapter, I present the experiences of Princess after her father was deported for a minor infraction during her 2nd-grade year and highlight the ways that undocumented status affects elementary school students, their families, and their teachers. I show how accessing and supporting families' immigration experiences requires cultivating relationships of mutual trust, a central component of humanizing family engagement.

Princess's parents, Federico (32 years old) and Cinthia (32 years old), were both originally from Puebla, Mexico, and met while living in New York City. Unlike most immigrant parents in Marshall, Federico had moved to New York when he was 9 years old, and Cinthia moved when she was in her later teens. Princess (8 years old) was born in New York, and when she was a toddler, her parents decided to move to Marshall for work opportunities and a less hectic life. During Princess's 2nd-grade year her baby sister, Brenda (1 year old), was born. Federico often dressed in a backwards Yankees cap or a Puebla York letterman jacket and could fluently converse, read, and write in English and Spanish from growing up in Mexico and the United States. He was a cook during the morning shift in a local restaurant so that he could care for his daughters most afternoons, when Cinthia worked cleaning hotels. Prior to Federico's deportation, Princess and Federico loved playing Xbox together, going to Chuck E. Cheese's, throwing a baseball in the backyard, and visiting their family members in New York.

Princess's experiences as a member of an undocumented family are not unique. In the United States, there are an estimated 5.5 million children who live in families with at least one undocumented immigrant, and 82% of these children are U.S. citizens (Passel & Cohn, 2011). This is equivalent to two students per U.S. classroom having undocumented family members (Suárez-Orozco, Yoshikawa, Teranishi, & Suárez-Orozco, 2011). Children from undocumented families attend schools throughout the United States, are not only Latin@, and include students of all ages. Thus, every teacher today, across every part of the country and level of schooling, is likely to work with a student who has undocumented family members. Yet, in preservice and inservice teacher education, immigration experiences and undocumented status are rarely broached, and teachers are left unsupported in understanding the dynamic realities of undocumented status and schooling (Gallo & Link, 2016; Jefferies & Dabach, 2014). Through the experiences of Princess, her family, and her teachers, I illustrate the tensions and possibilities of how teachers can foster a learning environment in which students can safely build upon their immigration experiences.

This chapter focuses on how educators can seek out ways for students to safely incorporate their immigration experiences into their classrooms. This is important because many students from this study who navigated life-altering immigration experiences (such as parental deportation) were searching for spaces and caring adults to share these experiences. Teachers were the adults children spent the majority of their day with and they often looked to their trusted teachers for support. In addition, schools are formative civic institutions in which young people develop notions of who they are and how they belong based on the ways ideas, practices, and types of people are understood. When aspects of difference, such as undocumented status, are continually silenced, it sends messages that those "without papers" are not part of our schools and communities. Many scholars have highlighted the importance of breaking these silences and the roles of educators in accomplishing this. For example, Dabach (2015) illustrates how a high school teacher's careful breaking of silence regarding an undocumented student who had been apprehended by immigration officers opened up spaces for students with different statuses to understand undocumentedness in humanizing ways. Maintaining silence perpetuates students' invisibility and leaves unchecked notions that being a member of an undocumented family is, as a Latina student in Marshall put it, "a bad thing."

However, looking to break these silences does not mean students should be forced to disclose their family's documentation status, a right the Supreme Court protected under *Plyler v. Doe* (1982) so that children would not be denied schooling as a result of their documentation status. It means, instead, that teachers should foster opportunities for students to draw upon their immigration experiences if and when they are comfortable doing so. Educators should be prepared to break the silence about undocumented status and schooling, but to accomplish this, they must also establish relationships of mutual trust with their students and their families.

PRINCESS'S LEARNING ACROSS HOME AND SCHOOL CONTEXTS

Princess was a spunky 2nd-grader in Ms. Vega's class who loved playing outside, watching kids' programs in English on TV, and negotiating *amiga/enemiga* (frenemy) relationships with peers. Her outfits were often fun and trendy, and it was common for her to arrive at school wearing a black shirt with a sparkly butterfly, black tights, white cutoff shorts, and mid-calf high-top Converse sneakers. Having attended a bilingual preschool, she tested out of ESL at the beginning of kindergarten. She excelled academically during her first years at Grant Elementary, but by 2nd grade she began to struggle in several subject areas. She was insecure about her academic abilities and oscillated between energetic participation and withdrawal during classroom activities. She thrived when given the chance to lead other children—such as guiding newly arrived students in their classroom or helping with her baby sister at home.

Prior to his deportation, Princess's father, Federico, was primarily responsible for Princess' schooling because of his work schedule, his well-developed bilingualism and biliteracy, and his greater familiarity with U.S. institutions. He engaged in many home-based engagement practices that were valued by Princess's teachers. Every day after school, he went through his daughter's backpack to locate pertinent handouts, helped her with her homework, and talked to her about her school day. Because of his English fluency, he attended most parent–teacher conferences on his own, including Princess's 2nd-grade conference that occurred hours after her baby sister was born. In the winter of 2nd grade, he also realized that Princess could not read and write in Spanish, something that her cousins who attended bilingual education programs in New York could do. He decided to begin teaching her Spanish literacy once their sleep schedule improved with the new baby, because he believed it was important for his children to develop literacy in both languages. He had high expectations for Princess's schooling trajectory: He regretted leaving high school after the 10th grade, and like many other fathers from this study, he talked to his daughter about the importance of going to college.

IMMIGRATION POLICIES AND SCHOOLING

As the lyrics of Princess's rhyme—"I don't wanna go to Mexico no more, more, more"—suggested, Federico and Princess considered the United States their home, and they never anticipated moving to Mexico. Federico had lived two-thirds of his life in the United States, and it was the country where all his friends and nuclear family lived. He differed from many immigrant parents in Marshall who had lived in the United States for only a few years and sometimes considered returning to Mexico because of the discrimination they faced as undocumented immigrants, separation from family members who remained in Mexico, or the deportation of their loved ones.

By the winter of 2010, Marshall had implemented immigration programs such as Secure Communities and the Immigration and Nationality Act, Section 287(g), which allowed local police officers to contact immigration authorities when they believed someone they stopped or arrested did not have U.S. documentation, as mentioned in Chapter 5. Under these immigration enforcement programs, Marshall transitioned from a relatively welcoming town for newcomers from Mexico to one where Latin@ adults were highly susceptible to deportations for minor infractions. Each family had stories of a close friend or family member who was stopped and sent to immigration authorities, and almost all the stories were about Mexican men, not women. Mothers in Marshall were rarely targeted for arrests and, if taken in, they were commonly released to care for their children. It became clear that local immigration practices disproportionately centered on Mexican men, and many fathers explained how they had become hyper-visible to local police officials. The consequences for interacting with local police were not predictable: Sometimes interactions did not lead to deportations, such as Mateo's encounters with the police (Chapter 5), but at other times they did.

Many families highlighted how immigration enforcement programs like Secure Communities created a context in which they felt they could no longer trust the police. Abi's father, Mateo, highlighted, "Instead of feeling safe with the police, we're even afraid of them." Many immigrant parents in Marshall discussed how they agreed with the premise of enforcement programs, which claimed to identify and remove undocumented immigrants who were the most serious criminal offenders. Parents wanted safe neighborhoods to raise their family and agreed that dangerous criminals should be deported. Yet their lived realities provided a perspective that differed from the stated goals of these deportation programs: These programs often deported Mexican immigrant men who had committed no crime other than being undocumented. This skewed enforcement led to a culture of fear for many immigrant families with undocumented members.

Fathers at Grant Elementary described how this increased vigilance impacted daily life for them and their families. As many scholars have emphasized, the stress of immigration practices does not just impact those who are deported; everyone living in undocumented families experiences the daily possibility of deportation or familial separation if a family member is deported (Brabeck, Lykes, & Hershberg, 2011; Suárez-Orozco, Yoshikawa, Teranashi, & Suárez-Orozco, 2011). Every family I knew had a plan for their children if the parents were taken by immigration authorities, and families tried to minimize their risk by literally staying inside their homes. Many fathers went out of their way to ensure that they were abiding by the laws because they knew one small misstep, such as an unpaid parking ticket, could lead to their arrest and deportation. They also knew that their deportation would not only change their lives, but their children's as well.

FEDERICO'S DEPORTATION AND PRINCESS'S SCHOOLING

Federico's Deportation

One Wednesday afternoon, I joined students for recess and Princess told me in a whisper that she had to speak with me. As we stood next to the swings, she told me in Spanish that the police had taken her father the night before and that he was going to return to Mexico. Her cousin, also a 2nd-grader at Grant Elementary, explained that she had seen Federico being handcuffed and put in a police car. This happened right outside their homes. As Princess's eyes started to well up with tears, we decided we would go to a classroom to eat in private. Over a lunch of *taquitos*, Princess shared her fears and uncertainties about what would happen to her father, and if she herself might have to move to Mexico, a country she had never been to.

That evening I spoke with Princess's mother, Cinthia, and learned that Federico had signed his automatic deportation to return to Mexico because the family did not have the financial resources to pay for bail and an immigration lawyer, which they had been told by other immigrant families would cost at least $10,000. Cinthia explained that Federico had been standing on the sidewalk in front of their home and had dropped a soda bottle as a police cruiser was driving by. This meant that police officers could fine him for the minimal infraction of littering and then send his information to immigration officials. They did this, which ultimately led to his deportation. Although Federico had lived in the United States since he was a child, he did not have official U.S. documentation. In the aftermath of the deportation, Cinthia emphasized how what her husband had done was just a little thing—nothing bad or terrible. She lamented how these little things can change everything.

Federico's deportation process highlights the blurred lines between being undocumented, which is often called "illegal," and criminality. Federico was moved to an immigration holding facility that was located within a prison, yet the basic rights often given to prisoners—such as the right to legal representation—were not granted to immigrant detainees. For the next 3 months, Federico was moved around to different immigration holding facilities before he went before a judge. During this time, Federico and Cinthia were in regular phone contact, a costly endeavor within the detention center calling system that charged nearly a dollar a minute. During the calls, they arranged the details of his return to Mexico, a country where he had no friends or close relatives. They also figured out how to get their children Mexican passports in case the entire family decided to return to Mexico. Both children were U.S. citizens who could also become Mexican citizens because Mexico was their parents' birth country. Federico learned they would also need detailed school records if they wanted to enroll their children in Mexican schools. Federico spoke with Princess, but did not want her to visit him in the detention center, where he looked like an inmate. Similar to 90% of those who were deported under Secure Communities (Kohli et al., 2011), Federico was not released prior to his deportation, and did not have the chance to say good-bye to his family.

Life and Learning at Home

Eight-year-old Princess's responsibilities regarding family–school engagement changed with Federico's absence. Cinthia had to take on additional jobs in order to make ends meet and she was often gone during most of Princess's waking hours. Although she would call Princess during her breaks and they had a close relationship, Princess was lonely, bored, and sometimes scared to be home alone. She took charge of her own homework completion as well as responsibility for the barrage of information sent home from her school each week, often translating the materials for her mother. Like other children in Marshall, Princess enjoyed translating these written texts into spoken Spanish, and worked collaboratively with her mother to complete these literacy tasks. In many ways, this literacy activity was more complex than many of Princess's school-based literacy practices, as it required her to navigate a wide range of genres, engage with written and oral media, and provide explanations across linguistic borders (Orellana, Martínez, Lee, & Montaño, 2012).

Federico's deportation also created new necessities for Princess's Spanish literacy development. The family's separation across borders cemented the possibility that Princess might have to attend school in Mexico, where she would need to develop Spanish literacy to succeed. During their phone calls from the detention center, Federico coached Cinthia on how to teach Princess to read and write in Spanish. Their separation also created real-world opportunities for biliteracy practices. Princess had been a reluctant writer, but written letters were one of the few ways she could correspond with her father once he was taken by immigration authorities. She would bubble with excitement each time she received a letter from him, and she started borrowing my notebook during school to write her father short letters in English, such as "Dear Dad. I love you so much dad." Eventually, she started asking how to spell things in Spanish, engaging more directly with Spanish literacy practices. These practices were not incorporated into the school-sanctioned literacy curriculum; instead, they occurred in the margins of the classroom.

Federico's deportation marked a major change in Princess's childhood: Cinthia described how she now talked with Princess like an adult rather than a little girl. Because of this deportation incident, Princess went from a stable two-parent household with academic support to a single-parent household in which Princess took on many new responsibilities. Although some of the authentic literacy practices opened up new motivations for Princess's biliteracy development, these experiences were not recognized or built upon in her 2nd-grade classroom. In addition, Federico's deportation was difficult for Princess emotionally, and at the end of 2nd grade she shared, "I don't wanna go to Mexico. . . . I wish he can come back. . . . I don't like my life anymore." Princess deeply missed her father and the life she had when he was in Marshall. Like many children who have been separated from parents by deportations, she struggled with feelings of depression, abandonment, and fear, as well as increased economic hardship (Brabeck et al., 2011). Like many young students at Grant who were dealing with separations from their parents, she was searching for outlets to deal with these changes, especially in school.

Life and Learning at School

Second Grade. Princess became withdrawn, distracted, and easily upset in school after her father's deportation. She would get sad in class when things reminded her of her father and she would occasionally act up in uncharacteristic ways. Although academic problems, depression, anxiety, and behavioral issues are all common effects of parent–child separations as a result of deportations (Brabeck et al., 2011), Princess's teacher Ms. Vega did not know about Federico's deportation and therefore lacked important information to contextualize Princess's behavior. Ms. Vega knew that Princess was acting differently, but did not know why.

Cinthia and Princess, like most immigrant families I knew, initially decided not to tell teachers about Federico's deportation because they feared it would make them look criminal. They had not developed a trusting relationship with Princess's teacher and they did not know her stance on undocumented immigrants. Indeed, Ms. Vega was very supportive of challenges faced by immigrants, but knew little about immigration practices overall in Marshall, and did not know they were affecting students in her classroom personally. She wanted to support her students, but as a new teacher who was trained to view good teaching as methodological rather than interpersonal, she avoided personal topics with them. She was particularly fearful of discussing documentation status, or being "illegal," because she worried she could be at fault for not reporting it:

> Quite frankly, if something is illegal, I don't really want to know it because I don't want to be responsible for not saying something. . . . We're always told in our courses, "You find something out that's not legal in a public school, then you have to report it." . . . If you don't and they find out that you knew about something, that's illegal. . . .

Ms. Vega reasoned that learning about a family's "illegal" status was parallel to learning about other illegal behavior, such as child abuse, which she would have to report. *Plyler v. Doe* (1982) protects undocumented students' right to public education and states that school officials, including teachers, cannot require students to share their documentation status or information such as Social Security numbers. Teachers in Pennsylvania and most states are not legally required to report undocumented students to immigration enforcement.

In addition, *Plyler* does not prohibit students or families from sharing their documentation status with teachers, and actually protects them further if they choose to do so. In fact, if a teacher does learn about someone's undocumented status, he or she *should not* report it, as this would be in conflict with the *Plyler* ruling (Borkowski & Soronen, 2009). Immigration and Customs Enforcement has agreed that schools are "sensitive locations" where raids and deportations are prohibited, and under the Family Educational Rights and Privacy Act (FERPA), schools are prohibited from sharing a student's file with immigration agents if it may contain information (such as the absence of a Social Security number) that would reveal a student's immigration status (Immigrant and Refugee Children, 2016). Schools should be safe spaces for undocumented students and families.

Ms. Vega's confusion about immigration status and mandated reporting is understandable, as she had never learned about *Plyler* or how undocumented status is protected in schools. She emphasized that in her teacher education, including her preservice program, inservice professional development experiences, her master's degree program, and her ESL certification coursework, "You talk about cultures, you don't talk about immigration." Even though almost half of the students attending Grant Elementary were from immigrant families, no professional development had been offered to support teachers in how to navigate immigration status and schooling. Associating undocumented immigration and illegality left students like Princess searching for safe spaces and caring adults to share and write about the realities of her childhood after her father's deportation.

Third Grade. Princess's 3rd-grade teacher, Ms. Costanzo, illustrates how a teacher can foster trusting relationships to move toward humanizing family engagement and learn about students' immigration experiences. Ms. Costanzo was a 3rd- and 4th-grade classroom teacher in her 11th year of teaching. In her classroom, she viewed herself both as an expert and a learner. She regularly pushed beyond her own comfort zone to learn about students' lives and created learning contexts that built on their personal experiences. In contrast to most other teachers at Grant Elementary, several of her students did talk and write about immigration practices in her classroom.

Princess explained that she had developed *confianza* in Ms. Costanzo because her teacher had noticed how sad she always was at recess and wanted to help. Through this relationship, Princess and her mother, Cinthia, decided to tell

Ms. Costanzo about Federico's deportation. Ms. Costanzo attended to Princess as a whole child, caring for her as a person and not just a student. She created outlets for Princess to deal with the challenges of her father's deportation, such as getting her to meet with a group of students who had been separated from their fathers, accessing counseling services for Princess, and encouraging her to journal about and write letters to her father. Recognizing Princess's growing interest in Spanish literacy, she also had Princess join the school newspaper club as a member of the translation team, who worked with university volunteers to translate the student-run newspaper. Through these bilingual literacy experiences, Princess was able to draw upon and expand her home-based literacy experiences. Ms. Costanzo's visible role as a trusted advocate for Princess created a context in which other students also decided to share their immigration experiences. Although Ms. Costanzo was not Latina and did not speak Spanish, she created spaces to validate and encourage her students' knowledges and experiences related to immigration practices and found ways to have their knowledges contribute to their school-based academics.

Ms. Costanzo also struggled with the challenges of doing this. She explained, "What's really hard is that I don't have just these students . . . I don't want those kids to feel like outcasted, or God only knows but the other kid goes home and tells someone." In a context of heightened deportations, she was aware of the potential consequences of having students share these experiences. Ms. Costanzo recognized the nuances in talking with students about such experiences and drawing on them in the classroom in ways that signaled to students that they were welcome, but not required to share. Her relationships with students involved mutual trust as well as high expectations for their academic potential, rather than pitying them and expecting little from them academically (see Link, Gallo, & Wortham, in press). Ms. Costanzo recognized the benefits of bringing home matters into the classroom and found ways to build on them for learning, a central goal of humanizing family engagement.

ENVISIONING HUMANIZING FAMILY ENGAGEMENT: MUTUAL TRUST

Princess was not the only student impacted by changing immigration policies that criminalize immigrants for minor infractions. More than half of the students I worked with in Marshall navigated the potential or real deportation of a loved one or stressful encounters with enforcement officials. These experiences form part of the knowledges that they bring to their schooling, and to access these experiences, educators should seek out ways to foster relationships of mutual trust with students and their caregivers.

To develop trusting relationships, it is important for educators first to consider why discriminating against undocumented status is often acceptable.

Undocumented status is a type of social difference, just like race, gender, sexual orientation, and class, among others. For most other types of social difference there are laws, policies, and trainings to address processes of discrimination and injustice in schools, as imperfect as the execution of such policies may be. In contrast, it is often socially acceptable to discriminate against people based on their undocumented status or to silence dialogue around documentation and immigration. To build trusting relationships with immigrant families and students, it is important to consider how undocumented status is a type of social difference that merits dialogue and understanding.

Breaking Silences and Mutual Trust

By 2013, many immigrant families in Marshall decided to break the silence surrounding undocumented status in the larger community, media, and schools. After the mistaken arrest of another father from this study that led to his detainment, his wife decided to share their story in a set of white papers denouncing local enforcement and with local media outlets in both Spanish and English (see Gallo & Link, 2015). She decided to talk to educators at her children's schools and to break the silences about undocumented status that positioned immigrants as criminals.

As teachers at Grant Elementary learned more about local deportations, many sought out ways to build trusting relationships with students and their parents. They also named the challenges of teaching in a rigid, skills-focused schedule and finding time to foster personal relationships with students and families so that they would be able to tap into their diverse experiences and resources. Ms. Costanzo lamented this tension, saying, "I think that block is being under so much pressure to be their teacher and teach them, that the time is a huge obstacle." Educators at Grant believed that greater agency as teachers in the form and content of their pedagogy could foster opportunities for them to better understand and leverage their students' real-world experiences for learning, including their immigration experiences.

Expanding Classroom Spaces for Students' Immigration Experiences

Educators need support and guidance to figure out ways to safely incorporate immigration experiences into their classrooms. Currently, the topics of immigration and undocumented status are silenced within most teacher education programs and professional development. This leaves teachers unsupported in navigating how to create safe spaces for students' immigration experiences. Educators such as Ms. Vega are excellent teachers who have been taught to focus on methods and avoid the personal. Yet such impersonal approaches to teaching and learning do not work for young people like Princess. Students like Princess are searching for spaces to make sense of major life changes, to critically examine and deconstruct the messages saturating the media that say undocumented immigrants are criminals, and to know they are valued, important, and not alone. As Jefferies and Dabach (2014) argue, as teacher education programs increasingly emphasize diverse learners and equitable schooling, teacher education must go beyond understanding immigrant students through a linguistic lens and account for differences as a result of documentation status. This requires preparing teachers to be aware of political and ideological issues in working with students across all forms of difference, including documentation status. Rather than accepting the status quo of silence around issues of difference such as immigration, teacher educators need to foster dialogue and exploration as they prepare educators for the realities they will face in classrooms.

Students and families are likely to be more trusting of educators who signal an accepting stance toward undocumented immigrants and their experiences. The American Federation of Teachers (AFT) published a 2016 resource guide for educators working with immigrant and refugee children that provides practical ways that teachers can achieve this. These include distributing "Know your Rights" materials[1] to all students, visibly participating in National Coming Out Day in support of undocumented students on November 12 and partnering with local organizations to host workshops on immigrant rights.[2] Such actions signal to all students that it is unacceptable to discriminate based on immigration status. In daily practice, this also means educators must have the courage to speak up every single time a student negatively positions someone because of his or her national origin, heritage language, or family documentation status. It is especially important for teachers to engage in these courageous acts within a political climate in which discriminatory speech and actions are embodied and sanctioned by political leaders.

Opening up safe spaces to bring in immigration experiences does not mean that teachers should force children to talk about them: Certainly, some students will not choose to divulge this information, no matter what the classroom context or interpersonal relationship. Instead, it means promoting classrooms where a larger range of resources and experiences is welcome, safe, and valued for learning across types of (in)equities, if and when children would like to incorporate them. The experiences children have as members of undocumented families shape a part of who they are, but being undocumented is not their essentialized identity. Opening up safe spaces means proactively signaling that you, your classroom, and your school are spaces that will support undocumented families, their knowledges, and their experiences.

At Grant Elementary, some teachers became more interested in finding ways to bring immigration experiences into their curriculum once they built trusting relationships with families and began to understand these experiences. They became interested in determining ways to incorporate these topics through literature, writing prompts, and the social studies curriculum. Although immigration stories occasionally appeared in their school-sanctioned reader, these were examples of families immigrating with their papers. Many immigrant students from undocumented families noted that these immigration narratives did not resonate with their personal experiences. Instead of taking such an approach, teachers could intentionally include children's literature that creates spaces to reflect upon general immigration experiences (such as Shaun Tan's *The Arrival*, 2007), border crossing and family separation (for example, Duncan Tonatiuh's *Pancho Rabbit and the Coyote: A Migrant's Tale*, 2013), and possibilities for co-alition building across communities of color (for example, Tonatiuh's *Separate Is Never Equal: Sylvia Mendez and Her Family's Fight for Desegregation*, 2014). Teachers could also seek out curricular opportunities to develop their students' ideological clarity about undocumented status, helping them develop the critical skills to question the detrimental stereotypes that pervade the media and communities.

Many teachers also went to one another for advice, although outside of the migrant education director, most were relatively new to understanding experiences related to immigration and schooling. Rather than navigating undocumented status in whispered conversations, interested teachers could form inquiry groups where they bring their experiences, questions, resources, and ideas. By establishing a codified space to engage in this educational work, teachers can move undocumented status and schooling out of the shadows to the forefront of the educational work that they do. They could invite people from local universities, immigrant families, and community organizations to collaborate with them in learning about the ways immigration status shapes their students' educational lives, and how teachers can proactively and productively draw upon these experiences in their classrooms. For Princess, and the 5.5 million children from undocumented families in U.S. schools, this could help foster locally responsive ways to build upon students' immigration experiences to support their schooling goals.

PEDAGOGICAL TAKEAWAYS

- *Plyler v. Doe* (1982) makes clear that all children are guaranteed a public education, including those without U.S. documentation. Teachers should not report a student's or family's documentation status.
- Educators should actively signal an accepting attitude toward undocumented families. They can host Know Your Rights workshops or participate in National Coming Out Day for undocumented immigrants (AFT, 2016).
- Educators should be attuned to discriminatory comments regarding undocumented status, national origin, or language within their classroom and should intervene every time such comments are made.

- Educators can incorporate literature that relates to immigration experiences, such as books by Duncan Tonatiuh.
- Several recent documentaries are excellent resources that highlight undocumented students' educational experiences. Ben Donnellon and Tatyana Kleyn have created two short films that are available online and include bilingual curriculum guides: *Living Undocumented: High School, College and Beyond* (http://livingundocumented.com) and *Una Vida, Dos Países: Children and Youth (Back) in Mexico* (http://www.unavidathefilm.com/#introduction-1).

REFLECTION QUESTIONS

1. What opportunities have you had to explore the role of immigration status in students' schooling during your teacher education or in schools?
2. If Princess were your student, how could you open up spaces for her to talk and write about her immigration experiences in your classroom?
3. The explicit policies and implicit practices regarding immigration status and schooling are dynamic and complicated.
   a. What questions do you have?
   b. How can you locate resources to answer them?
4. In many spaces today it is socially acceptable to overtly discriminate against people based on real or perceived documentation status. What ideas do you have about how to work toward a goal of recognizing immigration status as a form of social difference that can be incorporated into educational spaces?

Chapter 7

Toward Humanizing Family Engagement

This book has looked specifically at the roles that Mexican immigrant fathers play in their children's educations to illustrate the importance of developing humanizing school policies and practices that proactively create spaces to recognize and build upon all families' educational contributions. Through this lens, this book has shown how nonmainstream caregivers' educational resources are largely invisible when measured against narrow definitions of what counts as parent involvement and learning in school today. These examples are not meant to dismiss teachers' efforts to build collaborations with diverse parents. Instead, they highlight that the status quo does not support meaningful collaborations with minoritized families, and that educators deserve and need more support to navigate these relationships. This final chapter explores the possibilities and challenges of adapting a humanizing family engagement framework with minoritized caregivers and students across schooling contexts.

HUMANIZING FAMILY ENGAGEMENT WITH CAREGIVERS

Through the experiences of fathers like Mateo, Julio, Cristián, Ignacio, and Federico, I have argued that a humanizing approach to family engagement would more effectively support students' learning than traditional standards- and assessment-based methods and curricula. Humanizing family engagement requires educators and caregivers to proactively find ways to learn across their differences. Educators, who are predominantly White and middle class (Ingersoll & Merrill, 2012), benefit from larger systems of power and privilege that have historically valued their approaches to schooling and discounted those of diverse families. Because of this imbalance of power, it is up to educators to take the lead in fostering humanizing relationships with students' caregivers. Inequities do not fix themselves, and it is unlikely that these collaborations will unfold by chance. Doing this requires intentionality and work. These collaborations matter because they provide a way for educators to better recognize and leverage the educational resources that students and their caregivers bring to schooling. In this chapter, I return to the four facets of the framework (what counts, ideological clarity, teachers as learners, and relationships of mutual trust) and offer practical suggestions for how educators can begin to adapt them with families in their local context. Orienting to a humanizing approach to family engagement is not all or nothing—it is a process that educators can dynamically adapt that will look and feel differently across spaces and time.

What Counts

Humanizing family engagement is an intentional departure from one-size-fits-all parent involvement policies that expect minoritized parents to abandon their pedagogies of the home and replace them with school-sanctioned educational practices. Educators' understandings of fathers at Grant Elementary may have been different if they had been encouraged to develop humanizing family engagement and had been given the space and resources to engage across difference to learn from students and their families. Teacher education programs should prepare future teachers to develop clarity regarding what counts as learning and engagement and to learn from diverse students and parents. Rather than focusing on a restrictive understanding of learning, programs should prepare teachers to determine pathways to achieve schooling goals based on their students' resources.

Education policies and school administrations often emphasize "improving parent involvement," especially for families who are not White and middle class. Most parent involvement initiatives for minoritized families entail programs, such as the Head Start program model, that attempt to teach diverse caretakers to take on teacher-like roles and make their homes more school-like (Baquedano-López, Alexander, & Hernandez, 2013; Gallo, Wortham, & Bennett, 2015). Rarely do they place the expectations or provide the resources for educators to question their own assumptions about good teaching or family–school engagement, or for educators to spend time with students' families to learn from them.

School administrators can move toward humanizing family engagement by:

- dedicating inservice training time to critically examine what your school means by parent involvement and how to achieve these goals collaboratively with minoritized families;
- providing interpreters at family events and contacting universities and religious organizations if professional interpreters are not feasible;
- providing training on how to work with interpreters and increasing the length of multilingual conferences so there is adequate time for discussion and translations;
- minimizing the documents educators are required to share with families during school events, and carefully examining the technical jargon and presupposed U.S. schooling knowledge that these documents demand for understanding;

- dedicating inservice training time for educators to visit students' homes as learners or to engage in neighborhood walks to learn about local resources;
- establishing mentoring programs in which teachers are provided with professional development opportunities to shadow educators who enact innovative and successful engagement practices with minoritized families (Ishimaru, 2014);
- developing community engagement teams in which diverse groups of students, parents, teachers, and community members come together to review the school's program model, involvement expectations, and homework policies to offer alternative approaches (Scanlan & López, 2015);
- creating a family resource room within the school, as a place that parents can freely spend time, meet, and engage in grassroots opportunities to support their children's education (Dyrness, 2011);
- carefully examining your school's sign-in and volunteer procedures with an eye toward how they would be experienced by undocumented caregivers; for example:
  - ➤ Imagine how processes that require taking a visitor's photo may be intimidating to those who fear official processes;
  - ➤ Recognize that undocumented parents cannot obtain state or FBI background checks to volunteer in their children's school, and examine if there are alternative measures that would permit caregivers to volunteer while maintaining students' safety; and
- examining the language practices of school events and decisionmaking groups, such as parent–teacher associations and school boards and doing the following:
  - ➤ Make sure those who speak languages other than English have access to these spaces and feel welcome there.
  - ➤ Purchase a district set of translation earpieces or provide interpreters.
  - ➤ Address messages that caregivers may receive because they do not know English, such as monolingual English-speaking school members showing frustration when languages other than English are utilized.

To begin to expand what counts as involvement, educators can do the following:

- Focus on what students do well, not what they do not do in school-sanctioned ways:
  - ➤ Talk to students or their caregivers about how they learned this practice.
  - ➤ Think creatively about how it could be leveraged to meet school-based academic goals.

- Relocate family–school events to important places in students' communities in an effort to spend time with families engaged in meaningful activities that are part of their lives.
- Get to know a subset of families better each academic year, in ways that are appropriate in your local setting:
  - ➤ Educators in my courses select one or two focal students to get to know personally. They spend time with them and their loved ones in families' preferred spaces. Educators enter those spaces as a learner.
  - ➤ Selecting a subset of students is not meant to offer them special treatment. Instead, it is meant as a way to get to know families in a manageable way.
- Invite caregivers into your classroom to teach something that matters to them:
  - ➤ Invite children or other family members to translate for caregivers who speak other languages, validating both multilingualism and the skill of translation.
  - ➤ Think creatively of alternative times and spaces that fit within the flows of families' lives, not the school schedule.

Ideological Clarity

Developing ideological clarity can be difficult for members of the dominant society because it requires regularly questioning what we have always assumed to be unquestionably true. This relates to privilege, or systematically conferred dominance, in which the beliefs and values of the dominant group are perceived as normal and universal (Sensoy & DiAngelo, 2012). Most people who do not identify as members of the dominant group, on the other hand, are often very aware of multiple beliefs about the world and the hierarchies of how they are evaluated. They know this because they have experienced discrimination for not embodying the dominant ideology. The challenge, then, is for teachers to figure out what their blind spots are and how to begin to question the ideologies they hold as unquestionable truths.

As someone who largely identifies as a member of the dominant group, an approach I take with my own ideological clarity is to be attuned to when I make assumptions—whether those assumptions are that something is normal, good, or bad. I examine what my assumptions are, why I make them, and how there may be alternative explanations or perceptions. For instance, when I learned from immigrant parents that they had left their children in the care of extended family members when they immigrated to Pennsylvania to work, my initial reaction was somewhat negative. I found myself wondering, as a nonparent at that time, "What type of parent would leave their child in someone else's care?" Probing my own reaction, I came to realize that I was raised to see "family" as nuclear family, and the thought of being raised by anyone other than my parents seemed "wrong." It didn't fit within the dominant ideology I had of family or "good parenting." Yet this is just one ideology of family and parenting, and a very privileged one. Because I am a middle-class person from the United States, it would have been almost impossible for my family to be in the same situation as my students' parents, who felt the only way they could feed their children was by moving to another country for work—a key reason many immigrant parents made these tremendous sacrifices. I also realized that the trust among extended family members for childrearing is something I do not benefit from in my own White middle-class family.

Educators can work toward developing ideological clarity by trying the following:

- Get to know people who have had different life experiences and openly learn from their perspectives:
  - ➤ If you notice yourself evaluating something about their experiences, kindly try to learn more about the meaning of these practices and question your own assumptions about what is normal.
  - ➤ Create a chart to separate observed practices from your reactions to them, as was described in Chapter 2.
- Spend time in places outside of your comfort zones:
  - ➤ These might be in nearby communities where students' families live or across national borders, through educator exchange programs.
  - ➤ Noticing how things are done and valued differently in other places can provide the space to question the ways you approach them.
- Take a class or workshop on antidiscriminatory education or implicit bias:
  - ➤ In universities, these courses fall under different names, usually with words such as *diversity, inequity,* or *multicultural* in the title.
  - ➤ Seek a course that takes an explicit critical stance in which students go beyond celebrating diversity to examine issues of power and privilege in education.
- Invite someone from a local organization out to coffee to learn more about resources, experiences, histories, and priorities in the local community.
- Start a book or documentary film club to join others in learning about ways to understand alternative histories and truths for families of color in your schools:
  - ➤ Possible books include Michele Alexander's (2010) *The New Jim Crow* and its accompanying website (http://newjimcrow.com),

Aviva Chomsky's (2007) *They Take Our Jobs! And 20 Other Myths About Immigration*, or Leigh Patel's (2012) *Youth Held at the Border.*

> ➤ Possible documentary films include Donnellon and Kleyn's (from Chapter 6), or other documentary films such as *13th* and *Underwater Dreams.*

Teachers as Learners and Relationships of Mutual Trust

I discuss these two components together because in real-world teaching and learning, they are often intertwined. For teachers to effectively engage in authentic collaboration with students and their families, they must understand themselves as both experts and learners. Most teachers are very comfortable seeing themselves as experts, as the ones who hold the answers and the ones who can evaluate how well students or family members demonstrate school-sanctioned forms of knowledge. Much more challenging is being open to learning from families and students and finding ways to leverage their knowledges and resources for school-based goals. This is hard work, but many scholars argue that it is a necessary approach to support students from minoritized backgrounds (Ladson-Billings, 1995; Paris & Alim, 2014).

For minoritized families and students to feel they can safely share their knowledges and experiences, they need to establish trusting relationships with educators. As Carol Lee (2007) emphasizes, learning is risky business, especially if you have largely been told that your knowledges do not matter for schooling. It is important to note that the value of *confianza* plays a central role in many Latin American communities, which may make it a particularly important approach for Latin@ families. As Gutiérrez and Rogoff (2003) emphasize, different individuals who are members of the same larger groups (often called cultures) have diverse histories of experiences and values. There is often overlap for members from a given cultural group, but there is also individual difference. For example, Mateo and Ignacio were both Mexican immigrant men, but they had individual histories and differed in how they approached building trusting relationships with teachers. African American caregivers at Grant Elementary had racialized histories of schooling that largely differed from Mexican immigrants' overall experiences, and there were important individual in-group differences among African American caregivers as well. This is why fostering interpersonal relationships matters—it requires moving beyond generalizations to understand and learn from individual people. This also requires recognizing that some people's experiences with dominant institutions—such as schools and the people who represent them—include a history of discrimination and distrust.

To begin taking on the role of learner and developing trusting relationships with families, teachers can do the following:

- Use one-on-one time with caregivers as a way to get to know one another rather than speed through a large amount of technical educational material.
- Prepare authentic questions to ask caregivers about their children and schooling and be intentional about building rapport.
- If there are materials that administrators require you to share with families, think creatively on how to make them conversational, or how to provide them to caregivers beforehand to minimize the time they take up during your conference.
- Be open to sharing about yourself in appropriate ways:
  - ➤ As an educator, you likely ask families questions about their lives outside of the classroom, which should be reciprocated by sharing about your own life as well.
  - ➤ What is appropriate will vary across contexts. Appropriate ways to share may include sharing interests about children's sports, as Mrs. Drescher did, or reciprocal sharing of hardship with loved ones, such as a teacher who shared her son's battle with cancer when Cristián discussed his wife's deportation.
- Seek out alternative forms of communication:
  - ➤ Ask families what their preferred method of communication is, offering examples such as phone, email, Facebook Messenger or private group pages, and so on.
  - ➤ Determine a system that can work for you and them, so that you do not have to relay each message through multitudes of platforms.
  - ➤ Set the goal of writing a handwritten card to a different student's family each week to name things that are going well.

When navigating relationships with families, it is useful to remember that caring relationships are about high expectations, not pity. Many families have navigated incredibly difficult circumstances with grace, and as you build trusting relationships with them, you will likely learn about tremendous resources as well as difficult experiences. These caring relationships should be accompanied by high expectations and collaborative support to help them meet their educational goals, not low expectations and pity for the difficult circumstances they have navigated (Valenzuela, 1999).

Humanizing Family Engagement and Minoritized Caregivers

In this book, I have argued that teachers should approach family–school relationships as humanizing engagement because it provides a lens to better recognize and pedagogically leverage the educational resources that diverse students and families bring to their classrooms. My focus has been on the experiences of

Mexican immigrant fathers because of their invisibility as engaged caregivers in schools and their hyper-visibilty as potential criminals under current immigration policies. However, humanizing approaches to family engagement do not just matter for Latino fathers. At Grant Elementary, African American families similarly were rarely positioned as contributing to their children's academic success.

As Cooper (2009) highlights, "the discourse and scholarship pertaining to the educational involvement of African American caregivers usually starts with discussions of parental *absence* rather than presence" (p. 381, emphasis in original). Many scholars have shown the important ways that caregivers engage in their children's schooling by teaching them to recognize and resist school-based racism in their classrooms (Kirkland, 2013), develop a healthy self-image in an environment that often discounts their abilities (Greene, 2013), and promote expectations of college attendance (Jeynes, 2010). These forms of parental engagement are often invisible to educators, but play significant roles in supporting minoritized students' educational success. Humanizing family engagement approaches provide the tools to begin to understand and uncover the ways educators often misread African American caregivers' educational practices, and how to begin to forge meaningful relationships and build upon them to meet schooling goals.

HUMANIZING FAMILY ENGAGEMENT AND EDUCATIONAL REFORM IN THE CLASSROOM

I acknowledge the importance of educational reform in meeting the needs of children from minoritized backgrounds at Grant Elementary. Yet, in solidarity with scholars who question one-size-fits-all approaches to schooling, I question whether current accountability measures centered on testing will improve educational outcomes (Huerta, 2011; Malsbary, 2016; Paris & Alim, 2014; Salazar, 2013). This paradox is alarming. Students in U.S. schools today are more diverse than ever, and they bring the largest range of linguistic and sociocultural resources to contribute to their school-based learning. But what counts as knowledge within schooling has become increasingly narrow, and accountability-driven pedagogies leave limited space to acknowledge and build upon the incredible resources that students already possess, resources that they have often learned through pedagogies of the home.

Rather than focusing on what students lack—such as very specific types of sanctioned knowledge—the work of schools and educators should be to understand what students already know and how to build upon those knowledges. This kind of teaching entails adopting curriculum and pedagogies that recognize children's resources as well as creating a classroom context in which these knowledges can be safely shared (Lee, 2007; Orellana, 2009). As Genishi and Dyson (2009) aptly summarize, schooling needs to "embrace normalcy of difference" (p. 145). Such an approach to schooling would recognize that diversity is the norm in schools and would engage in pedagogies that recognize and leverage this, rather than eradicate it.

However, this is not the schooling environment in which most educators teach today. The task at hand entails developing strategies to enact humanizing pedagogies within the real constraints of the school day. Here are some thoughts on how to achieve this:

- Understand that education is political.
  - ➤ When you teach the mandated curriculum, you are being political by accepting and reifying the status quo.
  - ➤ It likely does not feel political, because it has become positioned as normal and natural.
  - ➤ When you go against the dominant ideology of "good teaching," others may start to call you political. This is because you are pushing against powerful ideologies.
  - ➤ Both approaches to education—contributing to the status quo or striving toward change—are equally political.
- Develop ideological clarity.
  - ➤ The mandates around what you teach, and how you teach, are not the only or best ways for teaching and learning to occur.
  - ➤ By developing clarity that these are ideologies that dominate current schooling, you can begin to explore and imagine alternative approaches.
  - ➤ Christine Malsbary (2016) provides a clear illustration of how a group of educators came together to refuse the mandated testing that they viewed as harming their immigrant students. Her article offers strategies for how educators can organize against harmful policies and practices.
- Find the wiggle room in the curriculum.
  - ➤ It will be difficult to design a unit on translation and literacy if you are required to teach an entirely scripted literacy curriculum.
  - ➤ Look for ways to get creative about the materials and resources you can integrate, such as children's literature on immigration or current events around Black Lives Matter, and ways to make multilingual resources available and valued in your classroom.
- Foster interpersonal relationships with students to learn from them.
  - ➤ This is not the message of schooling today, and it may not be valued or rewarded by administrators.
  - ➤ Yet students at Grant Elementary repeatedly emphasized that this mattered for their schooling.
- Don't do it alone.
  - ➤ Look for like-minded teachers who are seeking ways to incorporate their students' knowledges into their teaching.

> Form monthly inquiry groups where you can gather around food to share questions, successes, and resources.
> Become part of a community of educators who can sustain and support the challenging educational work in which you are engaged.

- Be courageous and make pedagogical choices that do not conform to the mandated curricula.
  > When you know that what you are being asked to teach or how you are being asked to teach is damaging your students, seek out alternatives.
  > Look for mentors who have found ways to do this within your school or district to learn from and with them.
- Join organizations focused on humanizing approaches to schooling. A few examples include:
  > National Council for Teachers of English (http://www.ncte.org)
  > Rethinking Schools (http://www.rethinkingschools.org/index. shtml)
  > Teaching Tolerance (http://www.tolerance.org)
  > Teaching for Change (http://www.teachingforchange.org)

HUMANIZING FAMILY ENGAGEMENT IN A CONTEXT OF ANTI-IMMIGRANT SENTIMENT

Family Separation Across Borders

I end with a story about immigration, the subtext that shaped many students' educational lives. The summer after students' 2nd-grade year I received a phone call from Cristián, Emily's father. Emily's mother, Paloma, had taken her two U.S.-born children to meet their relatives in Mexico and to bring her older daughter back to live with them in Pennsylvania. Emily and her brother were U.S. citizens and could fly back to Pennsylvania, but her mother and older sister were not, which meant they had to pay a human smuggler upwards of $10,000 to cross the border. As an immigrant without papers, Paloma had not been able to safely cross the border to see her daughter for almost 9 years. Although the family knew it was dangerous, they decided crossing the border was a risk they had to take for their entire family to be together.

I had anxiously been awaiting news from Cristián. As I answered the phone, Cristián's usual upbeat demeanor gave me hope, and I thought he was calling with good news. I soon learned he was not. When attempting to cross the border, Paloma had been apprehended. She had used someone else's identification to cross, which was charged as a felony and meant she would be imprisoned for several months in Arizona before having to return to Mexico. Her daughter, however, had successfully crossed the border and was en route to Marshall. Cristián asked for my help enrolling her in school, something he was uncertain how to do because, as her stepfather, he was not her legal guardian. I called a trusted friend who worked for migrant education. She was a tremendous resource and advocate in Marshall schools, and she helped Cristián enroll his newly arrived daughter. Like other parents who wanted to break the silence about the ways undocumented status was affecting their children's lives, Cristián had candid conversations with his children's teachers so they could understand the significant changes in their lives.

Immigration Reform and Schooling

In 2014, the Department of Homeland Security discontinued Secure Communities and similar immigration programs. Many of those deported under such programs were not criminal offenders—they were community members who had arguably been targeted by police officers for minor infractions such as littering and traffic violations, or simply because they opened their doors to police officers. This does not mean, however, that mixed-status families are now safe. New immigration policies and programs are regularly introduced, targeting specific subpopulations of undocumented immigrants, which reignites a culture of fear among immigrant families. The 2016 presidential elections, in which Donald Trump regularly dehumanized Mexicans and undocumented immigrants and suggested increased deportation programs, brought increased levels of fear to many Latin@ immigrant families.

Immigration policies contributed to a context in which Cristián became a single father raising two daughters and a young son. On top of his responsibilities, he carved out time to present at local academic conferences to share his experiences and perspectives with educational researchers and teachers. At one conference in 2015, he emphasized the importance of breaking the silence about deportation policies by urging immigrant parents to talk to teachers about parental deportations and family separation. He noted that teachers are busy and it is a lot to expect them to have 35 *corazoncitos* (little hearts), one for each of their students, inside their own hearts, which are already so full of joys and challenges. Yet he worried that ignoring these realities, and not working together to support children's schooling, would negatively impact students' academic trajectories.

During the conference presentation in 2015, other immigrant parents shared the emotional roller coaster of recent immigration initiatives. One mother had arrived a year too late to qualify for Deferred Action for Childhood Arrivals (DACA), an immigration policy announced by President Obama in 2012 that allowed educationally successful, young, undocumented immigrants relief from deportation and a pathway for legal employment. Other parents shared how they had cried tears of joy in 2014 when President Obama announced Deferred Action for Parents of Americans and Lawful Permanent Residents (DAPA), which would provide similar relief to parents of children who are U.S. citizens. But these tears of joy changed to fear and uncertainty when DAPA was blocked by state-level courts. Parents discussed the complex processes of hopeful anticipation and disappointment. They described how, as mixed-status families, they think they can see the light at the end of the tunnel, and then it is gone. Still, they hold onto hope, especially for their children and their educational futures. They are thankful for the caring educators who believe in their children, and who are invested in working with them to support their schooling. Yet these relationships take work, and many of these parents' engagement practices are not being fully leveraged for their children's schooling.

This book has shown that minoritized families are engaged in powerful educational work that traditional approaches to parent involvement and schooling often erase or discount. Humanizing approaches to family engagement provides a pathway to begin building interpersonal relationships with caregivers to openly question assumptions about what counts as knowledge, education, and involvement in support of students' academic goals. It is founded in the belief that we—as educators, teacher educators, and educational researchers—have a great deal to learn from diverse students and caregivers, and that schooling should be a reflection and expansion of their educational resources.

Case Study Children and Family Members (2010–2011)

Focal Child	Names and Relations	Birthplace	Age	Chapter(s)
Abi		Puebla, Mexico	8	Chapters 1, 3, 5
	Mateo, father	Puebla, Mexico	29	
	Susana, mother	Puebla, Mexico	26	
	Carlitos, brother	Marshall, PA	2	
Emily		Marshall, PA	8	Chapters 4, 7
	Cristián, father	Puebla, Mexico	30	
	Paloma, mother	Puebla, Mexico	27	
	Cristofer, brother	Marshall, PA	1	
	Cassandra, sister	Puebla, Mexico (lived there)	11	
Gregorio		Marshall, PA	8	Chapter 2
	Julio, father	Puebla, Mexico	29	
	Lucinda, mother	Guerrero, Mexico	30	
	Lily, sister	Marshall, PA	2	
Martina		Marshall, PA	8	Chapter 2
	Ignacio, father	Oaxaca, Mexico	36	
	Alejandra, mother	Puebla, Mexico	31	
Princess		New York City, NY	8	Chapter 6
	Federico, father	Puebla, Mexico	32	
	Cinthia, mother	Puebla, Mexico	32	
	Brenda, sister	Marshall, PA	1	

Two additional fathers, Daniel and Evaristo, also participated in this study, but do not feature centrally in this book.

Research Methodology

Data collection involved intensive ethnographic fieldwork and video recording of routine activities over the course of the 2010–2011 year in families' homes and students' school (see Gallo, 2013) for a detailed explanation of research methods). Home-based data collection entailed monthly participant observation of routine interactions, interviews with focal fathers and children, bimonthly home-based video recordings conducted by families using small handheld cameras, and playback sessions of these recordings. Home-based data provided a window into fathers' educational engagement in their children's lives, as well as how they fit within broader patterns of household practices.

School-based participant observations and video recordings occurred weekly within two focal classrooms as well as during school-based family events. During each half-day classroom visit, I focused on a single student from the study, following him or her across activities and interactions. I would sit near the student in order to observe and understand the school day from his or her perspective, including classroom and recreational activities such as lunch. When I was videotaping, which occurred during half of my school observations, the focal student would wear a lavalier microphone and the camera would be placed near him or her. During family–school events, I would serve as an interpreter between English-speaking teachers and Spanish-speaking parents. Interviews were also conducted with 2nd-grade teachers and administrators. School-based data provided a window into how students and teachers recognized, positioned, and built upon fathers' educational contributions.

As an English–Spanish bilingual, I collected data in the languages used by participants. For example, all interviews and playback sessions with fathers were conducted in Spanish, whereas all interviews with teachers were conducted in English. Children sometimes had monolingual interactions (just in English or just in Spanish) and also translanguaged in English and Spanish, which I would reciprocate. Out of respect for parents' home-based language policies and practices, during interactions with children in front of parents I spoke in Spanish, even when children translanguaged or addressed me in English.

DATA ANALYSIS

As I sat in classrooms and families' homes, I would jot down my observations and direct quotes in a small notebook. This served as the first line of analysis because what made it into the notebooks, and then into my fieldnotes, was based on what I noticed and deemed important related to my research questions (Emerson, Fretz, & Shaw, 2011). The night after each interaction, I would write up my fieldnotes from the different observations that day, highlighting what I observed in one section as well as my reactions or connections to these observations in a separate section. During data collection, I read through my corpus of data quarterly to bring together emergent themes, which I typed into conceptual memos (Heath & Street, 2008). The larger ethnographic study resulted in a large corpus of data: 221 fieldnotes (from participant observations), 75 video logs (from classrooms, homes, and conferences), and 47 audio logs (from interviews and playback sessions). It also resulted in 20 full interview transcripts: 7 from teacher interviews completed in English by an outside transcription company and 13 from father interviews completed in Spanish by my research assistant, a college freshman from a Mexican immigrant family in Marshall who was familiar with local varieties of Spanish. Transcripts of select interactions were also completed by my research assistant or myself, and then checked by the other.

My ethnographic analyses follow Emerson and colleagues (2011) and Heath and Street (2008), iteratively drawing patterns from the hundreds of fieldnotes, video logs, and transcribed interviews. After I completed data collection, my analysis included open coding using the qualitative data software program Atlas.ti. During this phase of analysis, I continually adjusted my coding scheme to reflect central themes and wrote additional memos that highlighted connections and inconsistencies I noticed among the data (Saldaña, 2015). The larger project resulted in 60 codes, including themes such as "fatherhood," "literacy practices," and "immigration." The key findings of this research study are presented within this book.

CONTINUED RELATIONSHIPS

I completed data collection in the summer of 2011, and continued to spend time with students and families through 2013, when an academic position led me to leave Pennsylvania. My close friend and colleague, Holly Link, continued working on ethnographic studies with the same cohort of students and families at Grant Elementary through 2014. Holly now works at RevArte, a grassroots organization in Marshall founded by Latin@ immigrants, which helps sustain my communication with many local immigrant families, including families from this study. Cellphones and social media have also provided a pathway for me to remain in contact with families, students, and teachers, and I return to Marshall for in-person visits annually, now with my own children by my side. Students—who I once knew as preschoolers and are now middle schoolers—continue to teach me how to learn across difference and strive for an educational system that recognizes and leverages their many educational talents.

Notes

Preface

    1. All participant names and locations are pseudonyms.

Chapter 1

    1. The first year of the study was conducted by Kathryn Howard, Holly Link, Miriam Fife, and myself. The second year was completed by Holly Link and myself. The third year, which is the focus of this book, I conducted alone.

Chapter 2

    1. I served as an English–Spanish interpreter at conferences at Grant Elementary school for 7 years. I do not have formal training as an interpreter, but I do have extensive experience in both Spanish and English engaging in educational activities. Families that I worked with through my studies often requested that I serve as the interpreter in their conferences. Teachers also knew me well because I observed classes weekly.

Chapter 4

    1. Metalinguistic awareness is also called metalanguage. Both terms highlight the importance of learning the "meta," or "about" how languages work. For consistency, I use the term *metalinguistic awareness*.

Chapter 5

    1. As an emergent bilingual in English and Spanish, Abi sometimes drew upon nonstandardized forms of English. These are represented in the transcription.

Chapter 6

    1. "Know Your Rights" documents provide tactics for undocumented immigrants and other minoritized groups who encounter police and immigration officials.

    2. This guide can be accessed at http://www.tabe.org/files/filesystem/ICE%20 Raids_Educators%20Guide%202016.pdf

References

Alexander, M. *The new Jim Crow: Mass incarceration in the age of colorblindness*. New York: New Press.

Alim, H. S. (2010). Critical language awareness. In N. H. Hornberger (Ed.), *Sociolinguistics and language education* (pp. 205–231). Bristol, UK: Multilingual Matters.

American Federation of Teachers (AFT). (2016). Immigrant and refugee children: A guide for educators and school support staff. Available at http://www.tabe.org/files/filesystem/ICE%20Raids_Educators%20Guide%202016.pdf

Apple, M. (2004). *Ideology and curriculum*. New York, NY: Taylor & Francis.

Arango, O., Flores, S., Gallo, S., Lara, M., Link, H., Arreguín, D., & Peregrina, I. (2016). *Un trago dulce pero adentro con sabor amargo* (A bittersweet swallow): Constructing counterspaces to explore undocumented status across academic, family, and community spaces. *Diaspora, Indigenous, and Minority Education, 10*(4), 1–15.

Arzubiaga, A., & Adair, J. (2010). Misrepresentations of language and culture, language and culture as proxies for marginalization: Debunking the arguments. In E. Murillo, S. Villenas, R. Galván, J. Muñoz, C. Martinez, & M. Machado-Casas (Eds.), *Handbook of Latinos and education: Theory, research, and practice* (pp. 301–308). New York, NY: Routledge.

August, D., & Shanahan, T. (2006). *Developing literacy in second-language learners: Report of the National Literacy Panel on language-minority children and youth*. Mahwah, NJ: Lawrence Erlbaum Associates.

Baquedano-López, P., Alexander, R., & Hernandez, S. (2013). Equity issues in parental and community involvement in schools: What teacher educators need to know. *Review of Research in Education, 37*, 149–182.

Barish, A., DuVernay, A., Averick, S. (Producers). (2016). *13th*. Available from Netflix.com

Bartolomé, L. (1994). Beyond the methods fetish: Toward a humanizing pedagogy. *Harvard Educational Review, 64*(2), 173–194.

Bartolomé, L. (2000). Democratizing bilingualism: The role of the critical teacher education. In Z. Beykont (Ed.), *Lifting every voice: Pedagogy and politics of bilingualism* (pp. 167–186). Boston, MA: Harvard Education Publishing Group.

Bartolomé, L. (2004). Critical pedagogy and teacher education: Radicalizing prospective teachers. *Teacher Education Quarterly, 31*(1), 97–122.

Barton, A. C., Drake, C., Perez, J., St. Louis, K., & George, M. (2004). Ecologies of parental engagement in urban education. *Educational Researcher, 33*(4), 3–12.

Borkowski, J., & Soronen, L. (2009). *Legal issues for school districts related to the education of undocumented children*. National School Boards Association. Available at http://www.nea.org/assets/docs/HE/09undocumentedchildren.pdf

Brabeck, K., Lykes, M., & Hershberg, R. (2011). Framing immigration to and deportation from the United States: Guatemalan and Salvadoran families make meaning of their experiences. *Community, Work & Family, 14*(3), 275–296.

Campano, G. (2007). *Immigrant students and literacy: Reading, writing, and remembering.* New York, NY: Teachers College Press.

Chávez, L. (2008). *The Latino threat: Constructing immigrants, citizens, and the nation.* Palo Alto, CA: Stanford University Press.

Chomsky, A. (2007). *"They take our jobs!": And 20 other myths about immigration.* Boston, MA: Beacon Press.

Chomsky, A. (2014). *Undocumented: How immigration became illegal.* Boston, MA: Beacon Press.

Cooper, C. (2009). Parent involvement, African American mothers, and the politics of educational care. *Equity & Excellence in Education, 42*(4), 379–394.

Dabach, D. (2015). "My student was apprehended by Immigration": A civics teacher's breach of silence in a mixed-citizenship classroom. *Harvard Educational Review 85*(3): 383–412.

Delgado Bernal, D. (2001). Learning and living pedagogies of the home: The Mestiza consciousness of Chicana students. *Qualitative Studies in Education, 14*(5), 623–639.

Donnellon, B. & Kleyn, T. (2014). *Living undocumented: High school, college, and beyond.* Available from http://livingundocumented.com

Donnellon, B., Kleyn, T., Perez, W., & Vásquez, R. (2016). *Una vida dos paises: Children and youth (back) in Mexico.* Available from http://www.unavidathefilm.com/#introduction-1

Doucet, F. (2011a). Parent involvement as ritualized practice. *Anthropology and Education Quarterly, 42*(4), 404–421.

Doucet, F. (2011b). (Re)constructing home and school: Immigrant parents, agency, and the (un)desirability of bridging multiple worlds. *Teachers College Record, 113*(12), 2705–2738.

Durán, L. (2016). Revisiting family message journals: Audience and biliteracy development in a first-grade ESL classroom. *Language Arts, 93*(5), 354–365.

Dyrness, A. (2011). *Mothers united: An immigrant struggle for socially just education.* Minneapolis, MN: University of Minnesota Press.

Emerson, R., Fretz, R., & Shaw, L. (2011). *Writing ethnographic fieldnotes* (2nd ed.). Chicago, IL: University of Chicago Press.

Epstein, J. (2010). *School, family, and community partnerships: Preparing educators and improving schools.* New York, NY: Westview Press.

Escamilla, K., Hopewell, S., Butvilofsky, S., Sparrow, W., Soltero-González, L., Ruiz-Figueroa, O., & Escamilla, M. (2014). *Biliteracy from the start.* Philadelphia, PA: Caslon Publishing.

Fenichel, M., Schweingruber, H. (Ed.). (2010). *Surrounded by science: Learning science in informal environments.* Washington, DC: National Acadamies Press.

Fogle, L. (2013). Parental ethnotheories and family language policy in transnational adoptive families. *Language Policy, 12*(1), 83–102.

Freire, P. (1970). *Pedagogy of the oppressed.* New York, NY: Seabury Press.

Freire, P. (1987). Letter to North-American teachers. In I. Shor (Ed.), *Freire for the classroom* (pp. 211–214). Portsmouth, NJ: Boynton/Cook.

Freire, P. (2001). *Pedagogy of freedom: Ethics, democracy, and civic courage.* Oxford, UK: Rowman & Littlefield Publishers.

Gallo, S. (2013). *Mexican immigrant fathers and their children: An investigation of communicative resources across contexts of learning.* (Unpublished PhD dissertation). University of Pennsylvania, Philadelphia, Pennsylvania.

Gallo, S. (2014). The effects of gendered immigration enforcement on middle childhood and schooling. *American Educational Research Journal, 51*(3), 473–504.

Gallo, S. (2016). Humor in father-daughter immigration narratives of resistance. *Anthropology and Education Quarterly, 47*(3), 279–296.

Gallo, S., & Link, H. (2015). "*Diles la verdad*": Deportation policies, politicized funds of knowledge, and schooling in middle childhood. *Harvard Educational Review, 85*(3), 357–382.

Gallo, S., & Link, H. (2016). Exploring the borderlands: Elementary school teachers' navigation of immigration practices in a new Latino diaspora community. *Journal of Latinos and Education, 15*(3), 180–196.

Gallo, S., Link, H., Allard, E., Wortham, S., & Mortimer, K. (2014). Conflicting ideologies of Mexican immigrant English across levels of schooling. *International Multilingual Research Journal, 8*(2), 124–140.

Gallo, S., Wortham, S., & Bennett, I. (2015). Increasing "parent involvement" in the new Latino diaspora. In E. Hamann, S. Wortham, & E. Murillo (Eds.), *Revisiting education in the new Latino diaspora* (pp. 263–282). Charlotte, NC: Information Age Publishing.

Garcia, E. (2002). Bilingualism and schooling in the United States. *International Journal of the Sociology of Language, 155–156*, 1–204.

García, O. (2009). *Bilingual education in the 21st century: A global perspective.* Malden, MA: Wiley-Blackwell.

García, O., & Kleifgen, J. (2010). *Educating emergent bilinguals: Policies, programs, and practices for English language learners.* New York, NY: Teachers College Press.

Gay, G. (2000). *Culturally responsive teaching: Theory, research, and practice.* New York, NY: Teachers College Press.

Genishi, C., & Dyson, A. (2009). *Children, language, and literacy: Diverse learners in diverse times.* New York, NY: Teachers College Press.

Gonzales, R. (2011). Learning to be illegal: Undocumented youth and shifting legal context in the transition to adulthood. *American Sociological Review, 76*(4), 602–619.

Greene, S. (2013). *Race, community, and urban schools: Partnering with African American families.* New York, NY: Teachers College Press.

Guerra, J. (1998). *Close to home: Oral and literate practices in a transnational Mexicano community.* New York, NY: Teachers College Press.

Gutiérrez, K., & Rogoff, B. (2003). Cultural ways of learning: Individual traits or repertoires of practice. *Educational Researcher, 32*(5), 19–25.

Gutmann, M. (1996). *The meanings of macho: Being a man in Mexico City.* Berkeley, CA: University of California Press.

Heath, S. B. (1983). *Ways with words: Language, life, and work in communities and classrooms.* Cambridge, UK: Cambridge University Press.

Heath, S. B., & Street, B. (2008). *On ethnography: Approaches to language and literacy research.* New York, NY: Teachers College Press, NCRLL/National Conference on Research in Language and Literacy.

Howard, K., & Lipinoga, S. (2010). Closing down openings: Pretextuality and misunderstanding in parent–teacher conferences with Mexican immigrant families. *Language and Communication, 30,* 33–47.

Huerta, T. (2011). Humanizing pedagogy: Beliefs and practices on the teaching of Latino children. *Bilingual Research Journal, 34*(1), 38–57.

Immigration and Nationality Act Section 287(g), 8 U.S. C 1357(g).

Ingersoll, R., & Merrill, L. (2012). *Seven trends: The transformation of the teaching force.* CPRE Working Paper (#WP-01). Philadelphia, PA: Consortium for Policy Research in Education, University of Pennsylvania.

Ishimaru, A. (2014). When new relationships meet old narratives: The journey towards improving parent-school relations in a district-community organizing collaboration. *Teachers College Record, 116,* 1–49.

Jefferies, J., & Dabach, D. (2014). Breaking the silence: Facing undocumented issues in teacher education. *Association of Mexican American Educators Journal, 8*(1), 83–93.

Jeynes, W. (2010). The salience of the subtle aspects of parental involvement and encouraging that involvement: Implications for school-based programs. *Teachers College Record, 112,* 747–774.

Jiménez, R., García, E., & Pearson, P. (1995). Three children, two languages, and strategic reading: Case studies in bilingual/monolingual reading. *American Educational Research Journal, 32*(1), 67–97.

Kirkland, D. E. (2013). *A search past silence: The literacy of young Black men.* New York, NY: Teachers College Press.

Kohli, A., Markowitz, P., & Chavez, L. (2011). *Secure communities by the numbers: An analysis of demographics and due process.* University of California, Berkeley: The Chief Justice Earl Warren Institute on Law and Social Policy.

Ladson-Billings, G. (1995). Toward a theory of culturally relevant pedagogy. *American Educational Research Journal, 32*(3), 465–491.

Lee, C. (2007). *Culture, literacy, & learning: Taking bloom in the midst of the whirlwind.* New York, NY: Teachers College Press.

Link, H., Gallo, S., & Wortham, S. (2014). 'gusame ka'lata!': Faux Spanish in the new Latino diaspora. In A. Creese & A. Blackledge (Eds.), *Heteroglossia as Practice and Pedagogy* (pp. 255–274). London, UK: Springer.

Link, H., Gallo, S., & Wortham, S. (In press). "*Que las maestras hablaran mas con ellos*": Children grappling with documentation status at school. In S. Salas & P. Portes (Eds.), *Latinization of K–12 communities: National perspectives on regional change* (pp. 123–140). Albany, NY: SUNY Press.

López, G. (2001). The value of hard work: Lessons on parent involvement from an (im)migrant household. *Harvard Educational Review, 71*(3), 416–437.

Malsbary, C. (2016). The refusal: Teachers making policy in NYC. *International Journal of Qualitative Studies in Education, 29*(10), 1326–1338.

Mangual Figueroa, A. (2011). Citizenship and education in the homework completion routine. *Anthropology & Education Quarterly, 42*(3), 263–280.

Martínez, R., & Morales, Z. (2014). ¿*Puras groserías?* Rethinking the role of profanity and graphic humor in Latin@ students' bilingual wordplay. *Anthropology and Education Quarterly, 45*(4), 337–354.

Martínez, R., Orellana, M. F., Pacheco, M., & Carbone, P. (2008). Found in translation: Connecting translating experiences to academic writing. *Language Arts, 85*(6), 421–431.

Mazzio, M. (Writer). (2014). *Underwater Dreams* [DVD]. Available from http://www.underwaterdreamsfilm.com

McCarty, T. (2002). *A place to be Navajo: Rough rock and the struggle for self-determination in indigenous schooling.* New York, NY: Routledge.

Moll, L., Amanti, C., Neff, D., & González, N. (1992). Funds of knowledge for teaching: Using a qualitative approach to connect homes and classrooms. *Theory into Practice, 31*, 132–141.

National Center for Education Statistics. (2013). The condition of education 2013: English language learners. Available at http://nces.ed.gov/fastfacts /display.asp?id=96

National Center for Education Statistics. (2015). The condition of education 2015 (NCES 2015-144), English language learners. Available at https://nces.ed.gov/fastfacts/display.asp?id=96

National Center for Education Statistics. (2016). The condition of education 2016: Racial/Ethnic enrollment in public schools. Available at http://nces.ed.gov/programs/coe/indicator_cge.asp

National Reading Panel. (2000). Report of the National Reading Panel: Teaching children to read: An evidence-based assessment of the scientific research literature on reading and its implications for reading instruction. Washington, DC: National Institute of Child Health and Human Development, National Institutes of Health.

Orellana, M. (2009). *Translating childhoods: Immigrant youth, language, and culture.* New Brunswick, NJ: Rutgers University Press.

Orellana, M., & D'warte, J. (2010). Recognizing different kinds of "head starts." *Educational Researcher, 39*(4), 295–300.

Orellana, M., Martínez, D., Lee, C., & Montaño, E. (2012). Language as a tool in diverse forms of learning. *Linguistics and Education, 23*, 373–387.

Paris, D., & Alim, H. S. (2014). What are we seeking to sustain through culturally sustaining pedagogy? A loving critique forward. *Harvard Educational Review, 84*(1), 85–100.

Passel, J. (2011). Demography of immigrant youth: past, present, and future. *The Future of Children, 21*(1), 19–41.

Passel, J., & Cohn, D. (2011). *Unauthorized immigrant population: National and state trends, 2010.* Washington, DC: Pew Research Center.

Patel, L. (2013). *Youth held at the border: Immigration, education, and the politics of inclusion.* New York, NY: Teachers College Press.

Plyler v. Doe, 457 U.S. 2020 (1982).

Salazar, M. (2013). A humanizing pedagogy: Reinventing the principles and practice of education as a journey toward liberation. *Review of Research in Education, 37*, 121–148.

Saldaña, J. (2015). *The coding manual for qualitative researchers* (3rd ed.). Los Angeles, CA: Sage.

Santa Ana, O. (1999). "Like an animal I was treated": Anti-immigrant metaphor in US public discourse. *Discourse and Society, 10*(2), 191–224.

Scanlan, M., & López, F. (2015). *Leadership for culturally and linguistically responsive schools.* New York, NY: Routledge.

Sensoy, Ö., & DiAngelo, R. J. (2012). *Is everyone really equal?: An introduction to key concepts in social justice education*. New York, NY: Teachers College Press.

Shatz, M., & Wilkinson, L. (2013). *Understanding language in diverse classrooms*. New York, NY: Routledge.

Shin, S. (2013). *Bilingualism in schools and society*. New York, NY: Routledge.

Soto, G. (1998). *Big Bushy Mustache*. New York, NY: Knopf Books for Young Readers.

Suárez-Orozco, C., Yoshikawa, H., Teranishi, R., & Suárez-Orozco, M. (2011). Growing up in the shadows: The developmental implications of unauthorized status. *Harvard Educational Review, 81*(3), 438–472.

Tan, S. (2007). *The arrival*. New York, NY: Arthur A. Levine.

Thomas, V., & Collier, P. (1997). Two languages are better than one. *Educational Leadership, 55*(4), 23–27.

Tonatiuh, D. (2013). *Pancho rabbit and the coyote: A migrant's tale*. New York, NY: Harry N. Abrams.

Tonatiuh, D. (2014). *Separate is never equal: Sylvia Mendez and her family's fight for desegregation*. New York, NY: Harry N. Abrams.

Tuck, E. (2009). Suspending damage: A letter to communities. *Harvard Educational Review, 79*(3), 409–427.

U.S. Department of Justice. (n.d.). Ensuring English learner students can participate meaningfully and equally in educational programs. Available at http://www2.ed.gov/about/offices/list/ocr/docs/dcl-factsheet-el-students-201501.pdf

Valdés, G. (1996). *Con respeto: Bridging the distances between culturally diverse families and schools: An ethnographic portrait*. New York: Teachers College.

Valenzuela, A. (1999). *Subtractive schooling: U.S.-Mexican youth and the politics of caring*. Albany, NY: SUNY Press.

Velez-Ibañez, C. (2010). *An impossible living in a transborder world*. Tucson, AZ: University of Arizona Press.

Villenas, S. (2002). Reinventing *educación* in new Latino communities: Pedagogies of change and continuity in North Carolina. In S. Wortham, E. G. Murillo Jr, & E. T. Hamann (Eds.), *Education in the new Latino diaspora: Policy and the politics of identity*. (pp. 17–35). Westport, CT: Ablex Pub.

Wortham, S., Murillo, E., & Hamann, E. (2002). *Education in the new Latino diaspora: Policy and the politics of identity*. Westport, CT: Ablex Pub.

Worthy, J. (2006). *Como si le falta un brazo*: Latino immigrant parents and the costs of not knowing English. *Journal of Latinos and Education, 5*(2), 139–154.

Zentella, A. C. (2003). "José can you see": Latin@ responses to racist discourse. In D. Sommer (Ed.), *Bilingual games* (pp. 51–66). New York, NY: Palgrave Press.

Index

About the Author

Sarah Gallo is an assistant professor of bilingual and immigrant education in the department of teaching and learning at The Ohio State University. As an anthropologist of education who conducts ethnographic research across Latin@ immigrant children's schools, homes, and communities, she critically engages in promoting school-based learning that better recognizes and builds upon young children's mobile and heterogeneous resources in the United States and Mexico. Her current research, which examines repatriated students' educational experiences in Mexican schools, is supported by the Fulbright Scholars Program and the National Academy of Education and Spencer Foundations. Her research has been published in journals such as the *American Educational Research Journal* and *Harvard Educational Review*. She holds a PhD in educational linguistics from the University of Pennsylvania.